BUILD YOUR BLOG STEP-BY-STEP:

Learn How to Create, Customize, Write, Publish and Promote
A Blog From The Very Beginning

JACOB GREEN

COPYRIGHT

Table of Contents

Before I start to share a step by step process to write a successful blog, I would like you to be aware of the pros and cons of blogging as well. Although Blogging can turn out to be a highly rewarding job. You might wonder about how come can blogging have any disadvantages or unfavorable things that one should know.

There are numerous instances of bloggers raking in huge profits – however, I wager they buckle down as well. Except if your blog thought has uncommon needs, you can work from anyplace whenever. During these years I've likewise needed to adapt new things and face consistent difficulties, for example, SEO, email showcasing, content advertising, travel composing, experience sharing, and so forth. I've even met some energizing individuals in the business. You have total authority over your business bearing. Awful or great, you are the one making major decisions. It's satisfying to compose a bit of content realizing that it'll help many several individuals. Particularly on the off chance, you get positive input.

You'll see a lot of individuals flaunting how a lot of money they are making with their blog. Nonetheless, know that not every person makes it. Except if your venture grows a great deal, you are well on the way to work independently from anyone else so it can feel segregating on occasion. You can generally join a cooperating domain to mingle. You don't need to be an alumni engineer. Be that as it may, running a blog requires some specialized information. In any event, you ought to be eager to learn. Know that making your own blog resembles beginning some other business. In the event, you are to be fruitful, you'll need to work more earnestly than your rivals. I haven't met anybody that was fortunate enough to begin bringing home the bacon from their blog in 2 months. I would state you ought to take a gander at 1 year before you start seeing a few outcomes.

A Step-By-Step Process That Goes From The Very Beginning To Have A Successful Blog

In the efforts or intention to be an effective blogger, you only need to consider one key factor i.e. enthusiasm towards the explanation of your point. Choosing a theme you would like to provide an explanation on or enthusiastic about any particular thing leads you to the development of a fruitful blog but make sure to keep it simpler. Illuminating on no less than the point is considered fine. You might sometimes require more time on one particular topic or things of your inspiration which would surely assist in intriguing your reader.

Apparently, there is no need for credentials, years of experience to be a professional content writer or school degrees in terms of starting a blog and becoming successful in it.

You might have heard of a lot many key factors before, but have not read much detail about them. Thus, the key factors that you need to consider are mentioned below to get started with your blog.

1. Pick a blog name:

The first and foremost step in getting started with the blog is to choose a good name for your blog. A lot many people have told you that you need to have expertise about the topic of your blog. But, that's not true at all! Your interest to write about any topic is enough to get started and learn things about it and increase your knowledge. If you have chosen the widely searched topic, then you probably have the chance of getting much traffic on your site. An increase in the blog traffic would allow you to earn money.

When you have a subject it's an ideal opportunity to pick your blog name. A decent blog name ought to be spellbinding with the goal that potential readers can in a flash determine what your blog is about just from the name. On the off chance, you are intending to make an individual blog where you examine an assortment of subjects then I suggest utilizing your name, or some variation of it since your blog is about you. some blog name thoughts you should pick a domain expansion.

A .com domain augmentation is the most liked, however, .net or .organization function also. It is likewise imperative to take note of that for the reasons for a blog domain you can't have any domains between words. So "Lead the way" becomes leadtheway.com. Along these lines, how about we begin with picking your blog's name. In the event, you are making a blog since you need to impart information to other people, you need to at any rate know more than the essentials of the subject you have decided for your blog. Put yourself from your readr's point of view and attempt to keep them straightforward and noteworthy.

2. Get your blog on the web.

Since you have a name chosen it's an ideal opportunity to get your blog on the web. This may sound hard or specialized, however, the means beneath will walk you directly through and make the procedure simple. You likewise need to choose which web facilitating administration you are going to profit off. The numerous Webhosting specialist co-ops have different rates and costs, with relating highlights: The measure of web domain they can give, The expense and method of installment, Customization and accessibility of instruments, and safety efforts set up, uptime, just as the speed of access. You'll see that costs extend every month, contingent upon whether you need a fundamental, single blog facilitating plan or a progressively hearty arrangement that enables you to make numerous sites.

The blog have I suggest, and the one I tell you the best way to use in this guide is BlueHost. One uses BlueHost and I suggest them for every single new blogger. Since they will enlist your blog name for you for nothing, ensuring nobody else can take it, offer a free, basic establishment of the WordPress blogging programming, have been suggested by WordPress since 2005 and presently have more than 2 million online journals and sites, accommodating every minute of every day client support through telephone or web talk and an unconditional promise on the off chance, you are unsatisfied in any way, shape or form.

When you do that you can pick an essential plan layout for your blog (you can without much of a stretch change this later).

3. Customize your blog.

When you sign in, you will be taken to your BlueHost Portal. From the entry, you can click "Sign in to WordPress" to be signed in naturally to your blog. Since you have effectively taken your blog to live, the subsequent platform is to structure your blog.

After the establishment, you more likely than not saw that your blog looks extremely fundamental. To make it all the more outwardly engaging, you'll need to introduce a topic. A subject enables you to pick a plan for your blog without the requirement for coding skills or structure information. As such, a great subject causes you to plan your blog precisely how you need it to look. In the event, you're not a coder (I'm unquestionably not a coder), at that point, a topic makes the plan work a million times simpler.

You can show up genuinely your own, by structuring and altering it to pass on the picture you'd like. On the off chance, you have your own blog intended for you or on the off chance, you make the introduction yourself, look for approaches to make your blog stand apart from the rest. At the point when you are choosing which subject to pick, ensure that you go for straightforwardness. It truly enables when you to have a spotless plan alongside great content. On the off chance, your blog doesn't look great, at that point, your readers won't try perusing your content, regardless of how great it is.

In the event, you don't care for any of the subjects that are now introduced, you can undoubtedly browse a huge number of other free topics. To introduce another subject, click on the "Appearance" tab on the left menu and afterward click "Include New Theme". There are a large number of topics to browse. You can change your whole structure whenever just by actuating another subject. To discover a topic you like, I recommend you click on the "Well known" tab and start perusing. At the point when you discover one that you like to tap the blue "Introduce" button.

Presently we're at the point in this guide where everything starting now and into the foreseeable future will be based upon the presumption that you've just enrolled your domain name and picked the privilege facilitating plan—so on the off chance, you haven't done so as of now, take only a couple of moments to rapidly get set up on Bluehost.

4. Write and disseminate your first post.

Composing a blog entry is a science. To us, it feels more like a maths condition than an English exercise since it must have such a large number of various criteria and fixings to fulfill the readr thus that it positions on a web index. There are unreasonably numerous fixings to a blog entry to expound on.

The thing you should think about composing a decent blog entry is that arrangement is fundamental. You need to research and structure your blog such that will fulfill any inquiries that your readr may have. You additionally need to have the privilege SEO recipe to guarantee that it is clear and that it positions on web crawler indexed lists.

We generally compose our web journals in WordPress. Like we said previously, composing a blog entry is an eccentric science and on the off chance, you need to get familiar with our effective equation.

5. Promote your blog.

The creation of a well-designed blog with high-quality content is only the starting point. If you intend to increase readers on your blog, you need to give more time to your blog for its promotion. However, there are a number of ways to get started to promote your blog, but each one would not suit best for you because it is all dependent on your content niche. An email has been one of the best channels of blog promotion.

Whereas on the other hand, the next thing to consider for blog promotion is social media like Facebook, Instagram, Twitter, LinkedIn, Pinterest, Reddit, and Snapchat. These are one of the biggest social media platform these days. Whichever platform is appropriate for your niche and interest of the audience is good for your blog. Promoting your blog on every social media platform might tend to be a pointless step. This is due to the reason that each network of social media supports a particular niche and reader.

Now and then when we advance another blog entry we will put a few dollars behind it to support its scope on the main day. Gone are the days when Facebook was anything but difficult to develop and your posts were seen by plenty of eyeballs. Presently they need your money for the benefit.

In any case, you need to move toward this in the correct way. Building connections is a two-way thing, and it begins with you giving.

- BuzzSumo – Find influencers in your specialty and find famous point thoughts.

- Constant Contact or Sendinblue – Start sending a normal email bulletin to your group of spectators.

- OptinMonster – Create popups and different battles to develop your email list.

- Buffer – Schedule your presents via web-based networking media on getting more blog traffic.

It's an ideal opportunity to fill your blog with content that will pull in guests and keep them returning. The great content isn't sufficient; it ought to be an incredible content.

Your content ought not exclusively to be incredible and innovative; they ought to likewise be convincing, important, and offer an incentive to your readers. What will they escape from your content? Will they gain information or ability from it? Will the content some way or another tackle an issue they may have?

6. Make money blogging.

It's presently the very first moment of your blogging professions and you are as of now searching for how to profit. You have to discover your readers, start building associations with them, shaping a network around your blog, and continue conveying esteem (as content) before quickly attempting to sell them on an online course, purchasing your independent administrations, or something else.

It takes difficult work. Be that as it may, numerous individuals who stay with it have earned side money which they've developed into low maintenance or full-time pay. There are a lot of websites (and video blogs) that make 5-6 figures every month.

Your long haul objective ought to be to adapt whether it's an inactive or dynamic salary or low maintenance or full-time pay. Be that as it may trust us as two individuals who have gone through three years taking a shot at our blog and now receive the rewards. You can make it as beneficial as you need it to be. There are a few different ways you can make money blogging, from selling your very own items or administrations to getting paid to compose audits of items on your blog. Be that as it may, the simplest method to profit from your blog is to sell the publicizing domain.

Offshoot showcasing: This involves utilizing plenty of connections from partaking organizations to get a portion of income when readers buy items that you suggest.

Google AdSense: By utilizing the Google AdSense module for WordPress you can consequently run promotions on your site. Google does basically everything.

Creating and selling your very own items: Your raid into a web-based business can incorporate digital books, online courses and email courses, and outsourcing items.

When you have a mainstream blog, promoters will dog you for the chance to publicize. The most ideal approach to exploit this circumstance is to utilize Google Adsense. They discover the publicists for you and you should simply put the Google Adsense code on your blog to begin running promotions. Google Adsense takes the entirety of the difficult work out of the procedure and just writes you a check.

It is important to note, the one and the only thing that stands out in your way to let you start the blog is you. It is so easy to say "I am quite busy" or "I do not have enough time or "I am tired from work". These are all no more than excuses that you make to yourself. Make efforts to get started to end up with a worth-talking blog. For the beginners, you are required to repost your blogs on Medium and make it a practice because it is the free site for not only readers but also for users. You can also search for any particular Publication on Medium that tends to be popular in your niche.

The Best Platforms To Build A Blog

You may be thinking to start your own blog, and it may be confusing for you to choose the best platform for blogging. It is thought to be an intense decision due to the existence of a number of blogging platforms. How would you come to know about the best platforms that are suitable for you? Therefore, here I am going to provide you with assistance by letting you know about the key pros and cons of the most prevalent locales of blogging.

And since blogging is considered as an art that is more than composing or photographs posting, determining the best platform with respect to your needs is significant. What you all need is the platform that may be difficult to use but provides you with every feature that is required for customization of the blog.

In case, you might have never written a blog, you will significantly need to choose the stages of the blog that oblige amateurs. And most of your time would be spent in choosing your HTML or CSS code. On the other hand, if you have blogged eve, the alternative ways for coding might be considered important to you. Get ready to decide which platform is for you.

WordPress.org/com

One of the most popular software of blogging – WordPress was started in the year 2003, WordPress now powers no less than 30 percent of all the webs on the internet. It is an open-source as well as a free blogging platform which is primarily built for blogging only. It might not be easy for beginners to set up and customize. Thus, the .org version of WordPress is known for the provision of a number of features which are thought to be its counterparts but is also known for the provision of additional features of customization for any blogger. Such characteristics of WordPress work well for those who tend to have complete control over the blog customization i.e. monitoring of traffic via Google analytics and free monetization of the websites. But this platform is not thought to be easy for beginners to be used in an effective manner but it also offers both free and paid options to learn WordPress.

This is the place Bluehost becomes an integral factor. In addition to the fact, it is modest (just $2.95 every month on the Basic arrangement), yet it additionally gives strong highlights, including a free domain name, 50GB of circle domain, unmetered data transmission, free SSL, and 100MB of email stockpiling per account. Right now, Bluehost is the least expensive reasonable WordPress facilitating you can discover there. Estimating begins at the Personal arrangement for $4 (€3.6, £3.1) month to month charged every year, which evacuates all WordPress promotion. There is additionally a complimentary plan accessible, which is appropriate for a noncommercial blog as there is WordPress publicizing and no chance would you be able to adapt it.

On the off chance, you need to make money blogging, go with WordPress. There's no better choice. You'll claim your blog and site and you'll have genuine adaptability. There is no contention here. It's the default content choice and runs 30% of the web which is as it should be.

There is increasingly set-up that you'll have to do without anyone else, similar to purchase a facilitating plan, for instance. This is the main drawback in my psyche, however, you don't need to be a specialist. WordPress.org sites perform well for site improvement (SEO for short). Web optimization is the act of making your blog rank high in web search tools like Google. The higher you rank, the more readers you get.

Open source implies you can mess with the code. The end result of this is your deal with the look and feel of your blog. It would resemble being responsible for the text style, shading, and picture on your physical book spread. The proviso is that you'll require some specialized expertise (or money to employ a designer) to exploit this adaptability.

Medium

Propelled in 2012, Medium has developed into a network of scholars, bloggers, columnists, and specialists. It is a simple to-utilize blogging platform with the restricted person to person communication highlights. Medium works a lot of like an informal communication site where you can make a record and start distributing your articles. After you join, you'll have a profile address this way: https://medium.com/@yourname. Be that as it may, you can't utilize your own domain. Medium offers various approaches to enroll.

Try not to need to recall one more secret word for one more record? Forget about it. Join utilizing one of your online networking accounts. Pick Google or Facebook. You'll at that point be approached to sign into your (Google or Facebook) account. When you approve Medium to get to your record, it will divert you back to Medium.

Readers can remark on other's posts, suggest posts and pursue and offer their top choices. The procedure resembles numerous other blogging stages with the exception of Medium has a slight wind on the remarking procedure. Readers can feature and centerpieces of the content and make their remarks in the edges.

Medium permits outsiders inserting from different locales around the web. Makers can insert recordings from YouTube or Vimeo. They can include content from Twitter, Vine, Instagram, and SoundCloud.

The platform is allowed to utilize. On the off chance, you have your domain, you can connect it to singular stories. Shockingly, you can't do likewise with client accounts. Medium is additionally a mainstream spot to give your content a subsequent life. Numerous individuals who have an essential blogging outlet re-post articles on Medium for extra presentation.

Notwithstanding the capacity to compose blog entries, it likewise accompanies restricted long range interpersonal communication capacities. You can remark on others' content and "like" it (prefers are classified "applauds" on Medium). The audience is incorporated with the stage.

Gator by HostGator

Gator is a web designer and blogging platform made by HostGator, the famous web facilitating organization that we use to have the WPBeginner site. Gator offers a drag and drop apparatus that you can use to assemble any kind of site including web journals, business locales, and even an online store. It's significant that you don't befuddle the Gator manufacturer with HostGator site facilitating. You can utilize HostGator facilitating administration to begin a WordPress blog as we have done.

There are three distinctive Gator site and blog manufacturer plans. The Starter plan begins at $3.84 per month and incorporates free facilitating, free domain name and SSL testament, the intuitive developer instrument, adjustable formats, site examination, and every minute of everyday support. The Premium arrangement begins at $5.99 per month and incorporates everything in the Starter plan in addition to need support. Ultimately, the eCommerce plan begins at $9.22 per month. It incorporates everything in different plans however offers online business usefulness too.

Nonetheless, on the off chance, you are searching for a non-WordPress across the board blog platform and facilitating the arrangement, at that point Gator is the ideal choice.

Blogger.com

Blogger is a free blogging administration by Google. It offers a snappy and simple approach to make a blog for non-technically knowledgeable clients. Blogger is one of the most punctual blogging stages in presence. It was first propelled in 1999 by Pyra Labs. Later in 2003, Google obtained Blogger and overhauled it as the item we know today.

This old-clock of blogging is free, simple to utilize and, in light of the fact, it was purchased by Google in 2003, entirely solid. Like some other blog stages, Blogger deals with any speed and facilitating requests. You even get an SSL security endorsement (normally upwards of $70) tossed in for nothing.

Online journals are facilitated by Google (somewhat like having the world's most dominant landowner), except if you pay for a custom domain. Your Blogger account is packaged in with your Google account. For straightforwardness, you should simply sign in with your Google subtleties.

Working with Google brings advantages. Adapting your Blogger page should be possible through Google AdSense, which will add applicable advertisements to your blog. This is a more direct course to income than with a web designer.

On the off chance, there is one platform that is simple for tenderfoots to utilize, it is Blogger. This is a free blogging platform that is easy to use for anybody simply beginning with a blog. With this stage, a client can simply type their content, including photographs and share. Blogger.com likewise lets clients alter HTML and add gadgets to blog, which many blogging destinations for tenderfoots don't offer. Blogger is a Google administration, so clients should have a Google account and may discover the Google-related additional items repetitive or futile for their blog. It is likewise one of the blogging stages that numerous bloggers develop out of once they become familiar with blogging since it doesn't have any overhaul choices.

Blogger has been around for what appears everlastingly and keeping in mind that it does not have the usefulness and plan alternatives of WordPress and a few other of the present well-known blogging stages, it costs literally nothing to utilize. Truth be told, the main cost you'll have with a Blogger blog is a custom domain, yet going this course is totally up to you.

Tumblr

The New York-based small scale blogging webpage was established in 2007 and has more than 400 million websites. Transferring content, from pictures to compact articles, is fast and simple... also free! In spite of the fact, there is a scope of paid formats accessible.

Like Blogger, however, the development openings are constrained. There's not a similar foundation accessible to utilize online life advertising, mess with designs or assemble a propelled blog page. Sponsorship up your Tumblr blog is additionally precarious. Tumblr is somewhat not the same as other blogging stages. It is a microblogging platform with informal communication highlights including following different web journals, reblogging, worked in sharing apparatuses, and the sky is the limit from there.

Probably the best element of Tumblr is that it is centered around the network of bloggers, so it gives an assortment of choices to sharing and reblogging content. The drawback to blogging on Tumblr.com is that it doesn't concentrate on content, however photographs, and GIFs. Visual bloggers will adore it, yet journalists might need to discover another platform to utilize. The possibility of the reblogging content may likewise need offer with bloggers, especially in the event, you are blogging material that you need to have full oversight over copyright and other such securities.

Like Blogger and a few other blogging stages, Tumblr is totally allowed to utilize it. There are costs for a custom domain and outsider subjects and applications, yet these are discretionary.

Much the same as a normal blogging stage, it gives numerous post arrangements to various kinds of contents. The thing with Tumblr is that it is only for individual use and wouldn't set up an incredible arrangement on the off chance, you have business-situated plans. It is oversimplified, offers essential customization choices and, similar to I said before, has, even more, an online life vibe. In spite of not being worked for business, it lets you show advertisements on your page, use partner connects, and coordinate your blog with Google Analytics.

SEO and How To Rank On Google

In the event, you claim, oversee, adapt, or advance online content by means of Google Search, this guide is intended for you. You may be the proprietor of a developing and flourishing business, the website admin of twelve locales, the SEO authority in a Web organization or a DIY SEO ninja energetic about the mechanics of Search: this guide is intended for you. In case you're keen on having a total outline of the rudiments of SEO as indicated by our accepted procedures, you are in fact in the correct spot. This guide won't give any mysteries that will consequently rank your site first in Google (sorry!), yet following the accepted procedures plot underneath will ideally make it simpler for web crawlers to slither, list and comprehend your content.

Significantly improved platforms are known to have increased more traffic with time leading to the success of the blog. With Search Engine Optimization, the searchers will not have the option to reach your website and all your efforts will provide you with no potential outcome. The optimization of the website requires a continuous change to stay updated with the advancement in technology. So, in order to raise the traffic on your site, you must keep your content updated.

Thus, Search engine optimization necessities continuously changing, and it tends to be difficult to stay aware of the most recent advancements. Be that as it may, on the off chance, you need your site to get traffic, you must be up to date.

Explore the "Inquiries" report

Site page improvement is in 2019 STILL about making a site page important and believed enough to rank for some random inquiry question. It's tied in with positioning for significant keywords as long as possible, on merit. You can play by 'white cap' rules set somewhere around Google, and expect to construct this Authority and Trust normally, after some time, or you can decide to disregard the guidelines and go full time 'dark cap'.

Without having a strong comprehension of your pattern keyword execution, you won't realize how far you've come and the amount you've improved. To start with, we should discover the expressions that you're practically positioning high for. It's in Google Analytics in this report: Acquisition > Search Console > Queries.

On the off chance, you aren't ready to get to this report, you most likely haven't associated your Search Console record to Google Analytics.

This report appears:

- All the expressions you rank for

- The number of times you've shown up on Google (impressions)

- The number of times your pages have been visited from these expressions (clicks)

- How high you rank for the expression (normal position).

Set an impelled channel

We're searching for phrases that effectively rank in Google, yet could utilize improvement. We have to utilize an

Advanced Filter to discover only the expressions for which we rank high, however not very high. The thought is that a page that positions more prominent than 10 is high on page two. This accepts there are 10 natural pursuit postings on page one, which truly isn't the situation, however, it's nearly enough for us to make this work. Nobody needs to rank on page two, however, the uplifting news is, high on page two is nearly page one. You're directly underneath a tipping point. This is a low hanging natural product!

Sort the report by rankings

Snap the section header "Normal Position" to sort the report. In reality, you'll need to click it twice so you can see the 11s at the top. Spare your separated, arranged Queries report as an alternate way. This will make it simpler to get to next time. Simply click the "Alternate route" connect over the report, name it and snap OK. Presently the report will be accessible whenever in the left side route of Google Analytics.

Tunnel through this overview, find explanations and avow the rankings

You'll rapidly see that this report shows some weird expressions. Things that appear to be unessential. Try not to stress over them. Each site positions for inconsequential expressions. Simply disregard them and continue looking.

This report may likewise show expressions that incorporate your image name. Avoid past those as well. Site design improvement is tied in with positioning and getting traffic from non-marked expressions.

In a perfect world, you'll discover some purchaser related keyphrases. Keep in mind, there are two sorts of keywords... If the entirety of your keywords are enlightening, you will, in any case, produce natural traffic, however, it might be hard to change over those guests to purchasers or individuals who share via web-based networking media.

Check how the articulation is used on the page

Start scanning for the expressions in Google to affirm your rankings. Presently you'll see that the "normal position" truly isn't equivalent to rankings. Now and then, you'll see yourself positioning higher than the report recommends. On different occasions, you won't see your site by any stretch of the imagination.

There is a great deal of purposes behind the inconsistencies.

- Your site may have more than one page that positions for the expression.

- Your site may rank in picture list items.

- Your site may rank distinctively today than the normal positioning over the date run in the report.

- Improve the page and exhibit the significance of the articulation

Site design improvement is tied in with demonstrating significance. We show significance utilizing on-page SEO best practices, which we'll abridge here.

Utilize the keyphrase once in the page title

This is the <title> tag, which shows up in the code, however not on the page itself. It shows up in the program tab and it's regularly the interactive connection in Google query items. In the event, your site is in WordPress, the titles might be overseen inside a module, for example, Yoast.

Preferably, the objective expression shows up toward the start of the title and expressions of the expression are kept together, without any words separating it.

Utilize the keyphrase once in the header

This is the <h1> tag, which is commonly the feature on the page.

Utilize the expression a few times in the body content

There is no enchantment number for keyword recurrence, however high positioning pages will, in general, belong, with 1500 – 2000 words. Keep in mind, Google is an exploration device worked by library researchers. Google adores content!

In the event, your page is 1500 words, all things considered, four to six cases of the expression feels regular. On the off chance, the page is short, don't make a decent attempt to cushion it up by including length. In any case, ensure the expression shows up all the key phrases.

Improve quality!

In the event, you need to build your Google rankings, you will likely make the best page on the web for that subject. Try not to attempt to deceive a robot. Do attempt to assist individuals with finding the data they're searching for. Remaining spurred and on-track with your blog content can be a colossal test. Working with an accomplice can consider you responsible for reliably distributing content.

Google wouldn't like to inform us everything concerning how to rank profoundly, yet it wants us to create important content. In that capacity, the hunt behemoth gives the point by point rules on what we ought to and shouldn't do, with an accentuation on the "shouldn't."

At this point you ought to get the possibility that each bit of content should be well-looked into, connecting with, precise, and important to your intended interest group. It's anything but difficult to accomplish this with an incredible article group or Outsourcingd assistance, yet how would you figure out what they ought to compose? Google looks at your individual pages for quality signs, and it additionally checks your site comprehensively to evaluate the profundity of your content and how well you're covering points identified with your business. The Hummingbird calculation made this conceivable by bringing semantic investigation in with the general mish-mash. This enables Google to think increasingly like a human and decide the motivation behind the content, past explicit keywords.

Construct all the more top-notch connects to your page. It's as straightforward as that.

There are huge amounts of approaches to do this: visitor posting, repeating your rival's connections, "high rise" third party referencing, seeking after unlinked specifies, and so on. As a rule, including inside connections is the fastest and best alternative in the event, it would seem that your page may just need a little lift. While fabricating more backlinks is altogether if your page authority (URL Rating) is truly enduring.

Hold up two or three days and check your rankings:

As far as I can tell, a couple of little changes can greatly affect rankings, particularly if the page wasn't all-around upgraded in the first place.

The total amount of time that is required in finding keyword and update the page take no more than 10 moments. Unsurprisingly, the results become visible in a few days. Considering the average time in which results are being displayed generally ranges from 90-180 days which primarily depends on the intensity of the competition of your particular industry and the use of popular keywords. Due to a number of reasons, here I am discussing some of the key factors to help you rank your blog.

At the point when you type an inquiry into Google, pages are chosen from the list as indicated by how well they coordinate with your particular question.

There is no careful equation for setting your site at the highest point of a Google search. Be that as it may, the following variables assume a key job in the positioning procedure: SEO, Domain Page, Keyword Competition, Quality of Keywords, and clean domain. So in case you're keeping up your page with great content, keeping your domain clear of any obscure alternate routes, and concentrating on low-rivalry keywords that will develop your online position... show restraint. You're en route.

Positioning higher on Google isn't advanced science. However, doing as such for certain keywords is more testing than others. That is the reason it bodes well to pursue rankings for uncompetitive keywords for which you effectively rank on the principal page. It's then only an instance of making sense of why you're being outranked and doing everything possible to fix those issues.

Top 10 positioning variables of google:

Rich outcomes, or rich bits, are query items that give 'bits' of data without requiring a client to tap on a particular connection. They're what you see at the highest point of query items, particularly because of inquiries. For instance, see this quest for 'Motion picture name'. Yet, web crawler rankings are not just about keywords; they're additionally about the nature of data.

1. A Secure and Accessible Website

Obviously, the first of our SEO positioning elements has to do with having the correct sort of URL. In particular, that is a URL that Google's bots can undoubtedly reach and slither. At the end of the day, Google must have the option to visit the URL and take a gander at the page content to begin to comprehend what that page is about.

2. Page Speed (Including Mobile Page Speed)

Page speed has been referred to as one of the fundamental SEO positioning variables for a considerable length of time. Google needs to improve clients' understanding of the web, and quick stacking website pages will do that.

3. Mobile Friendliness

While we're regarding the matter of versatile, portable agreeableness is another major SEO positioning variable. A bigger number of individuals utilize cell phones than work domains to get to the web, and that is one explanation there've been changes in how Google positions indexed lists.

4. Domain Age, URL, and Authority

Now and again, domain name matters. In spite of the fact, Google has punished careful match domains (those where the objective keyword is in the URL), that punishment is for the most part for nasty locales with slender content. With regards to internet searcher positioning variables, authority matters. As you'll see, that is generally a blend of extraordinary content (see the following tip) and off-page SEO signals like inbound connections and social offers.

5. Optimized Content

It's not just about the principle keywords either; it's additionally critical to incorporate terms identified with the fundamental terms individuals are scanning for. These are called LSI keywords. They give a sort of online word relationship to assist Google with realizing which results to appear.

6. Technical SEO

Use keyword states in page titles, which is the place Google first hopes to figure out which content is applicable to which search. You'll see the page title as the mainline of an item section. Where it's suitable, use pattern markup to mention to Google what sort of content you're delivering. This can likewise enable your content to show up in rich card passages other than answer boxes.

7. User Experience (RankBrain)

In the event, individuals land on your site, don't care for it, and ricochet away, at that point Google will believe it's not significant to their needs. On the off chance, enough individuals do this, at that point, you may think that it is progressively hard for your site to rank higher in query items. Conversely, if individuals navigate to your site page and stick around for some time, that discloses to Google your content is significant to their pursuit. So when you streamline titles, depictions, and content to get the snaps and convey an incentive on the opposite end, you can support your internet searcher positioning.

8. Links

Google utilizes inbound connections as one approach to help decide how legitimate and applicable your content is. Preferably, you need to have not many inbound connections from low-quality domains. You can locate your inbound connections utilizing an instrument like SEMRush or one of the keyword.

9. Social Signals

Google's legitimate word is that social offers are not an immediate positioning component. Connections from Twitter or Facebook aren't considered similar connections from other definitive sites. In addition to the fact, you need to have an internet-based life nearness yourself, yet you have to make it simple to share your content and enhance those social sign.

10. Real Business Information

This tip is significant for organizations focusing on specific neighborhoods. The nearness or nonappearance of business data is one of the most significant nearby SEO positioning elements.

The Best Niches To Build A Blog In

You love beginning a blog. However, you don't know what to expound on. Or on the other hand, possibly you have a thought, however, you don't know whether it will work. Sound common?

In case you're gesturing your head, you're certainly not the only one. Picking a blog specialty is perhaps the hardest piece of beginning a blog – it makes all the specialized stuff appear to be a cake stroll in the examination!

How do profit bloggers consistently encourage you to go get a specialty you are enthusiastic about rather than trying to say these are the main specialties you ought to consider. on the off chance, you truly need to bring home the bacon with your blog.

By making content identified with the most well known and productive topic, you can expand the odds you'll build up and furthermore have adaptation openings. In case you're planning to blog professionally, these viewpoints are critical.

You may have a million thoughts bobbing around your head. Or then again, you may be battling to think of only one. Regardless of what your barricade is, I'm here to assist you with focusing on the ideal specialty for your new blog. You'll gain proficiency with the three inquiries you have to reply to think of a blog specialty that you can develop, stay with, and possibly adapt not far off.

For what reason do you need a blog specialty, in any case?

All things considered, there's no Internet police that will come separate your entryway in the event, you don't adhere to your specialty. What's more, there are individuals who've discovered accomplishment with a progressively dissipated technique. Your readers aren't destined to be keen on every one of the themes you actually love. So except if you can make yourself the subject of the blog (which is conceivable, personality or you), it's hard to construct a group of people that way.

Then again, on the off chance, you stick to one point, you can ensure that individuals who are keen on one of your posts have a high possibility of being keen on the entirety of your other content, too.

A specialty centers around your blog's content. On the off chance, you choose to simply expound regarding any matter that rings a bell, your blog can turn out to be to some degree disordered. Guests will most likely be unable to comprehend what your blog is 'about,' and this can affect your standards for dependability. A few out of every odd blog has a specialty, and there is some discussion about whether or not a blog must adhere to a particular specialty so as to be effective. In any case, it is commonly recognized that specialties give some helpful characteristics to blog destinations.

All things considered, the blogging specialties underneath will, in general, give adoptees to a higher probability of having the option to live serenely off their blog's income. We've aggregated this rundown by investigating which specialties will, in general, get the most traffic and produce the most pay. In this way, in light of the interests of individuals, the most mainstream specialties to make a blog on incorporates the following:

Personal development.

Composing is entirely important expertise. In spite of the fact, there are some who think authors are brought into the world with such gifts, most bloggers will affirm that the craft of correspondence is found out through predictable practice. What's more, in spite of prevalent thinking, probably the most high-traffic web journals are written in a conversational tone.

These days, there is a developing enthusiasm for self-development and personal growth procedures. There is a developing number of books, articles, and sites managing these subjects.

It appears that individuals are turning inside them, to discover the answer to their issues. They look for information, methods, workshops, talks, and educators, who can show them the way. Individuals are starting to comprehend that personal development and self-development can improve the nature of their lives.

Sharing your life, contemplations, objectives, accomplishments, and disappointments will be a guide to your readers to get motivated! It's anything but difficult to share about hypotheses and reasoning, however, to make those affect your readers you have been a genuine guide to them.

Start with declaring an objective you need to accomplish with the cutoff time and update your advancement every once in a while.

Health and Fitness for Busy People.

One of the huge online niches is health and wellness to start your blog. It is considered as the fact, universal topics to which people all around the world are aware of tending to be the most profitable niche for the blog. And this is thought to be fine because through blogging you are in connection with a large group of people all around the world. While blogging about a blog is considered to be a highly profitable one, despite you may be talking to a small percentage of people all around the world.

The greatest advantage of the health and wellness specialty is that the audience is eager for data (quip exceptionally proposed). Individuals need answers to their issues, and they need them now. This is an extraordinary specialty for a website like Pinterest, where it's simpler to develop traffic for new online journals. Most health and wellness websites begin profiting with offshoot programs. The leading workers have their very own data item that understands their audience's particular needs.

Wells of helpful data, stories, tips, accounts, items, and thoughts, these sites can show you new activities and plans, answer any inquiries or concerns you may have, just as offering you a network to interface and cooperate with. Indeed, there are such huge numbers of online journals out there, you ought to have the option to discover one for each health and wellness need you. Obviously, with such a significant number of decisions, things can get overpowering and you may not realize where to begin. Thus, make it simple for the readers to open your composed blog and find the solutions to the inquiries that they may have been searching for.

In this way, beginning a wellness blog is an extraordinary method to remain propelled, monitor your advancement and offer your mysteries with the world. It doesn't make a difference what your identity is, or how to fit you may look, anybody can figure out how to begin a blog about wellness.

Language Learning Blogs.

There are the self-evident, ordinary focal points to communicating in an unknown dialect, for example, dazzling your companions, pivoting a date that is going severely and perhaps the most grounded feeling of pride and accomplishment that you can have. It can likewise open numerous potential profession entryways, not just as far as the scope of occupations yet, in addition, the scope of goals is to get a new line of work abroad.

As the world turns out to be increasingly more globalized, the interest for language speakers from organizations is on the expansion as they extend activities into new markets. These organizations, accordingly, need language speakers to fulfill the requests of their customers over the world. It is a lot simpler to develop an association with someone when you communicate in a similar language as them. You can essentially interface with them on an increasingly close to home level and achievement correspondence obstructions. In the event, you communicate in a similar language.

Having more than one language additionally opens up a universe of excitement – the capacity to comprehend global craftsmanship and writing can truly welcome our general surroundings. Learning another dialect has never been simpler. The measure of free online language learning devices is so shifted and top to bottom that you are coming up short on reasons to be a monolingual these days. Your composed websites can without a doubt give individuals direction about how to realize and what language to realize with sharing of your encounters.

Travel:

At the point when we're voyaging, it's not unexpected to become involved with thrilling moments, moments that basically can't be re-lived only for a brisk photograph. All in all, what would this be able to mean? It implies that those remarkable recollections can be effectively overlooked weeks, months and years down the track... But there is another approach to save those moments, and that is through composing a touring blog about them.

Expounding on a spot and contemplating your own photographs enables memory to stick in your brain and you discover you, you'll recall it in years to come. I find that on the off chance, I don't blog about a spot I can scarcely recall it a couple of years after the fact however composing everything down encourages it to stick in my memory.

There is a colossal travel blogging network that is well disposed, inviting and will share your adoration for movement. I've met a portion of my dearest companions through movement blogging and it's incredible to have individuals who you can talk with about movement without exhausting them to death. You'll likewise have a system of companions who are among the most-voyaged individuals on the planet which is immaculate when you're searching for some occasion motivation!

At the point when you're out having new travel encounters, it's a given that individuals back home will pose huge amounts of inquiries when you return... But on the off chance, you don't have a precise record of the occasions, you won't have the option to disclose to them the entire story – how everything truly occurred at the time.

Approaches to create $100 dollars in a single week

Expounding on the approaches to create increasingly more money has been a generally looked through theme nowadays. Since money is significant that you won't be penniless. It implies that you are not reliant on being utilized, living check to check and enduring maltreatment by your supervisor since you severely need your activity.

An ever-increasing number of organizations are getting into the content game. Some have a reasonable methodology, while others are simply getting on board with the fleeting trend and trusting it pays off down the line.

This has made a business opportunity for keen authors who can compose for a particular audience. These content-hungry organizations need articles, white papers, contextual analyses — the rundown goes on. What's more, they completely hope to pay for them.

Breaking into this market can be intense without a couple of contacts to kick you off, however, it's certainly feasible.

Be that as it may, with tolerance and difficult work you can set up a reputation of effective ventures and split away from the low-procuring masses. Money gives you opportunities and decisions. You can choose where and how you need to live when you have a decent salary or budgetary assets. Then again, when you don't have a lot of money, the decision might be something that you can't bear. The decisions accessible to you may not so much be decisions by any stretch of the imagination.

Picking a specialty for your blog can assist it with remaining engaged and significant to your readers. Be that as it may, for proficient bloggers, the choice could likewise impact your pay. Going into one of the more famous and beneficial specialties could make it simpler to gain a living.

It is important to note, the emergence of inspiration is mainly not from a vacuum. Despite the twisting and turning in the world that is rich with digital and media powered by photos and videos of Instagram, the blog is primarily driven through writing and the use of words.

With a sustained focus on the creation of high-quality and find the readers of your blog. You will surely start noticing people who consistently visit your blog and engage with your content. So, here the only thing you need to focus on is engaging your audience and building community.

Domain name, hosting and where to buy it and how to set your domain (DNS, etc)

Domain names, as well as web-hosting, tend to be two entirely different services. You might think of a domain name that matches the name of your street that assists people in finding and accessing the location of your web. A domain name is primarily the string of identification defining the realm of the administrative autonomy, authority or control through the entire network of the internet. The use of domain names in varying networking contexts and the specified naming of the applications and addressing the purposes.

The selection of the domain name is thought to be your first expression. This is based on the fact, the first thing that any visitor sees on the website is its URL. The good and attractive domain name creates a positive and an everlasting expression whereas any negative or unappealing name presents totally opposite outcomes. It is primarily known to influence search engine optimization. However, EMDs – Exact Match Domains have no more been considered as a necessity but the use of keywords still provides you a significant change to get your blog ranked. It mainly defines your brand as your domain name is the opportunity of branding your product. The right selection of the brand name increases the recognition of your brand.

Whereas the companies of web hosting sell or rent space through their servers to let you store your files of the website i.e. CSS files and HTML, images, documents, and videos. Such files take up much space but require to be stored.

Any individual is capable to create a website on the computer but until and unless one has not uploaded his files on the hosting server, no one would have the right to access the website. After the files have been uploaded, as the people type your domain name they will be directed to your site in the browser.

On the other hand, if you have not purchased the service of web hosting, you will not be able to set up your site completely. In short, registration of your domain name without any service of web hosting would of no use, your website will be left incomplete.

Importance of a Domain Name

Having a good domain name is important due to a number of reasons which mainly includes that if you ever decide to change web host, your domain would remain the same. The visitors of your website who are well aware of the name of your site would not be required to be informed about the change in the web host due to the reason that your site would still be at the same place. Thus, by typing the name of your website, they will be automatically directed to the new site.

Considering the fact, you run a business site then the domain name is known to provide you credibility. Some of the people will represent their willingness to do business with a corporation with no domain name of its own.

If you successfully get a domain name of your choice describing the name or business of the company, it will be easy for people to remember their name and would surely t return your site without consultation of the documents.

Factually, if you are looking for a good advertiser or sponsor for the website, the domain name would be of great use. It is expected to give your site an impression of respectability.

The time duration of the domain names is about one year and can be renewed each year from Domain Name Registrars. The time duration of choosing to buy your domain name can be done for more than one year. The purchasing and payment for web hosting can be done by a single provider. Due to the particular specification of each service, it is considered common to get separate hosting and domain.

After the registration of the domain name, you will get more than one DNS – Domain Name Servers. They are equivalent to the phone book of the internet for the maintenance of the domain name directory and translating them into Internet Protocol addresses.

Registration Overview

In order to get the domain name, registration of the domain name that you require with an organization i.e. ICANN through the registrar of the domain name. the Internet Corporation for Assigned Names and Numbers is the organization responsible for the management of the domain names and IP addresses on the internet. The categorization of ICANN in TLDs is as follows:

- Generic Top-Level Domains (gTLD)

- Country-code Top-Level Domains (ccTLD)

- Sponsored Top-Level Domains (sTLD)

- Infrastructure Top-Level Domains (iTLD)

Some of the most popular TLDs are generally generic

domains which are as follows:

- .com – Commercial
- .org – Commercial
- .net – Commercial
- .gov – U.S. government agencies
- .mil – Military
- .edu – educational facilities like universities

For instance, if you select a name such as domain.com, there is a requirement to go to registrar, pay a specified registration fee costing an approximate of US $10 to the US $s35 for that name providing you the right to the name of the year and renew it on yearly basis with same amount annually. Some of the web hosts will register the domain name and pay for free whereas others will do that for you but would require a registration fee.

If you want to know my preference then it would be to get your domain name registered by the domain name registrar other than a web host. I have heard of a number of stories of some of the less reputable web hosts who registered the domain name using their own name and making themselves the honor rather than yours.

Direct registration with the registrar of a domain name allows me to be sure that I am myself registered as the owner, the administrative and technical contacts. Being the owner of your domain name is vital in case of being replaced by someone else as the owner like a web host. The web host can always decide in charging you some of the exorbitant fee for the later use of the name and there is very few to be done.

Whereas other different contacts are considered less vital but tend to play an important part that depends on your registrar. For instance, for some registrars, the approval of the administrative contact is needed before a domain name is transferred out of a web host. In case of not being in contact with the owner, other technical contacts tend to be used.

Domain names vanish incredibly quick. Numerous individuals guarantee that all the great domain names are no more. I question that, however, it is presumably evident that most great domain names that are unmistakable of items and administrations have been taken. In the event, you need a domain name for your site, I propose you to act now, or face the anguish of having lost that name later. All things considered, US$10 (pretty much) for a year's responsibility for the name is somewhat modest when you understand that you're verifying a decent name for your site.

Purchasing a Domain Name:

There are various domain name recorders. Recorded beneath are only a couple:

1. GoDaddy

GoDaddy is another major facilitating organization that offers a free domain when you buy one of their facilitating plans. From Shared and WordPress facilitating, to VPS and Dedicated facilitating choices, GoDaddy has something for everybody. While highlights differ contingent upon the arrangement you select, all GoDaddy facilitating bundles offer a free domain, ensure 99.9% uptime, and give top-class every minute of everyday support.

GoDaddy is additionally a considerable domain name enlistment center in its own right, at present overseeing more than 78 million domain names. On the off chance, you buy a domain name (without facilitating), you will find that GoDaddy doesn't offer a free SSL endorsement or domain security assurance with its domain names. Be that as it may, you do get

- .com augmentation – $2.99/year (restores at $17.99/year)

- .org expansion – $11.99/year (reestablishes at $20.99/year)

- .net expansion – $13.99/year (reestablishes at $19.99/year)

- WHOIS Privacy – $9.99/year

- Email – $1.99/year (recharges at $4.99/year)

- Website Builder and Hosting – Free first month (recharges at $5.99/mo)

- SSL Certificate – Included with facilitating

2. Domain.com

Domain.com is one of the most mainstream domain recorders. As a certified domain supplier, Domain.com enables you to browse all the significant top-level domain expansions, just as more than 25 nation code top-level domains. All domains acquired from Domain.com likewise accompany...

- .com expansion – $9.99/year (restores at $13.99/year)

- .org expansion – $14.99/year

- .net expansion – $12.99/year (restores at $15.99/year)

- WHOIS Privacy – $8.99/year

- Google G Suite – $6.00/mo

- Web Hosting – $1.99/mo (recharges at $3.75/mo)

- SSL Certificate – $3.33/mo

- SiteLock security – $2.08/mo

3. Namecheap

Namecheap is another well known and regarded domain enlistment center. Offering a broad assortment of TLDs, Namecheap additionally gives a colossal system of DNS servers over the US and Europe, just as the top-quality day in and day out live talk support. Different highlights accessible with Namecheap domain name buy incorporate:

- .com expansion – $8.88/year (reestablishes at $10.88/year)

- .org expansion – $12.98/year

- .net expansion – $11.98/year

- WHOIS Privacy – FREE

- Google G Suite – $6.00/mo

- Email – Free for 2-months (restores at $3.88/year)

- Web Hosting – $1.28/mo (restores at $2.88/mo)

- SSL Certificate – $3.88/year

Most will offer limits and modest costs when you purchase a domain just because however when you reestablish it, the cost will be higher. On the off chance, you can manage the cost of it get it for over one year immediately. Since you need to develop your portfolio and online nearness, first attempt to get your very own name as a domain yet in the event, you can't, be imaginative and thought of something you realize you will use for a long while and it is significant.

Register or Setting up Domain Name

GoDaddy.com

Setting up a Domain Name with GoDaddy.com includes the following advances:

Platform 1: Go to GoDaddy.com and type your picked domain name.

Platform 2: When you see that your domain name is accessible, select the $2.99 alternative. At that point, select "Keep on trucking" on the upper right.

Platform 3: On the following screen, you can choose in the event, you need domain security insurance. On the off chance, you're not stressed over individuals realizing who claims the domain, at that point just select "Forget about it".

Select the term and continue to checkout.

Select for to what extent you need the domain to be enrolled, remember the most cost-effective term is as of now for a long time, this gives you a general 41% rebate.

In any case – when you've chosen your term, hit the "Continue to Checkout" button. When you've chosen a reasonable term, you will need to make a record, trailed by entering your installment subtleties. Furthermore, that is it, your domain is enrolled with you.

Domain.com

Platform 1: Open the Domain.com site inside your program and afterward type your picked domain name into the search function.

Platform 2: If your picked domain name is accessible, Domain.com will naturally add it to the shopping basket.

Platform 3: Under Shopping Cart select how long you might want to buy your domain for (of course this is set at two however can be as meager as one year or upwards of five).

Platform 4: Domain.com will currently attempt to sell you a determination of domain additional items.

Platform 5: You will presently need to round out your own data and afterward enter your installment information.

Namecheap

Platform 1: To set up your domain name with Namecheap, enter your picked name into the pursuit bar on the site's home page.

Platform 2: Namecheap will presently tell you which domain extensions are accessible, alongside the cost of each.

You will discover Namecheap is somewhat more forthright with estimating than huge numbers of the other domain registrars. As you will find in the picture above, just as the limited time costs, where suitable the reestablishment costs are additionally shown. This implies as it so happens you are sure about how much your domain name will cost you long haul.

When you have picked the privilege TLD for your domain name, select Add to Cart.

Platform 3: Namecheap will currently attempt and upsell a portion of their additional items and services.

Platform 4: Next, you can set the number of years you might want to buy your domain. (On the off chance, you have settled on a limited TLD, at that point the more extended term you pick the more drawn out your rebate will last).

Platform 5: Next you will be approached to make an account with Namecheap and enter some fundamental data including name, email, address, telephone number, and friends subtleties if suitable. At that point basically, enter your installment information and buy your domain name.

Contingent upon the length of your domain name term, you'll need to reestablish your domain name in a year, two years, or more.

It's significant that you make sure to do as such – something else, your domain name will go disconnected. What's more, on the off chance, you won't get on inside half a month, your domain name will return available to be purchased and another person can get it – not bravo.

Make a note to recharge your domain before it closes. Maybe a Google schedule update or an update from your cell phone. Whatever the case, ensure you remember.

For some domain name enlistment centers (like the ones we referenced above), you can set it to restore your domain toward the finish of its term consequently. This is the most secure alternative – simply ensure that you stay up with the latest (this can be anything but difficult to overlook).

In the event, you don't have a site yet, at that point 2020 is going to begin and is the best time to begin. What's more, the initial step to making your site is to enlist your domain name.

With this straightforward guide, you can enroll your domain name rapidly and effectively. Before you know it, you'll have your own little bit of the web.

General Tips And Tricks From Experts. Best Practices And Mistakes To Avoid

It is safe to say that you are attempting to get the outcomes you need from your blog? Blogging can be convoluted, so you need to ensure you're doing things right.

We asked our Social Media Examiner journalists "What's the single greatest mix-up bloggers make and why?" Read their answers cautiously to perceive how you can improve your blogging to get the outcomes you need. Following is a rundown of the most widely recognized blogging botches, which are effectively maintained a strategic distance from in case you're mindful of them.

SEO enables the motors to make sense of what a specific page is about, and how it might be helpful for clients. In the present significant level of rivalry, it is basic to be as high as conceivable in the list items, and that accompanies a productive SEO technique. Be that as it may, many aren't sure of how to rank another site on Google.

Google Loves Unique Content

What Google likes is extraordinarily remarkable content. We have seen the ascent in the significance of content creation and curation as a showcasing instrument in the course of the most recent couple of years. Individuals utilize the web to discover data that is the reason Google is putting such a high incentive on interesting content. Making extraordinary infectious content that asks to be shared, for example, recordings, blog entries, and digital books likewise have a major side advantage. That advantage is that individuals will connect to your site or blog and consequently Google gives you large ticks in its web crawler figuring are the more frequently back-joins are made to your blog and site from different sites.

Discover an accomplice you can be straightforward with:

Being available to new recommendations implies that you have to tune in with a receptive outlook just as feel-good giving and getting genuine criticism. While I could never say, the holy cow that sucks! I would state possibly you could utilize a greater amount of the blue you utilized a week ago or recommend an alternate text style so it's anything but difficult to read. There's an aptitude for giving positive evaluate and you need to work with somebody that will enable you to develop – not cut you down.

Tips to practice:

Do your blog entries feel a piece samey? Do they some of the time neglect to draw in the readr? Helping you to explore your way through the clamor with a rundown of Top things to maintain a strategic distance from when composing a blog entry...

Publish Relevant Content:

The first and foremost driver of the ranking of the search engine is quality content and it has no substitution. The creation of the quality content specifically for your target user increasing the traffic of the site improving the authority and relevance to the site. Thus, there is a requirement of fine-tuning the writing skills of the website.

Keywords:

Identification and targeting the specific keyword phrase for every page of the website. Consider yourself as the reader, and then think about how any reader would search with the specific use of key terms. It is considered quite difficult for a webpage for the achievement of the rankings of the search engine for multiple phrases of keyword until and unless such phrases would be considered similar. A single page upholds the ability to rank for both the biomedical engineering careers and biomedical engineering jobs. In context to this, the ranking for the dean of students and student affairs or gender discrimination and violence reporting procedures is not alike. If you wish to rank the multiple phrases of keyword with your website, there is a requirement to make a separate page of the website for each phrase of the keyword you would be targeting.

Placing Keywords:

After the placement of the keyword for a given page, consider the following questions as an example like:

- Can I use keywords in the URL of the page?

- Can I use keywords in the URL of the page title?

- Can I use keywords in the URL of the page headings and subheadings?

The answer to these questions is yes as it would significantly improve the ranking of the search engine. You need to be natural and user-friendly. For example, you do not need to use the word engineering any less than three times in the URL or have the repeated keyword such as Northern Lights on the title page and every heading. Usability and readability still trump search engine optimization.

Content:

Beyond the URL of the page, title, headings, as well as the content, is greatly influenced by the rankings of Search Engine Optimization. Repetition of the keywords as many as times as you can – one or two times in the closing and opening of the paragraphs and two to four times in the rest of the content. It is important to remember to use the bold, italics, heading tags and other tags that emphasize for highlighting the keywords but do not exceed. But make sure to keep your writing and language style naturally. Do not ever sacrifice on the good SEO writing. Also, keep in mind that the best content pages are written for the users not for the search engine.

Regular update of your content:

You might have noticed that quality content makes you feel strong as the same search engines. Regular update of the content keywords as one of the key aspects of the relevancy of the site to make sure that everything is fresh and updated. Auditing of the content on a set schedule and make updates as per requirement.

Metadata:

When considering the website designing, each page contains a specific space among the <head> for the insertion of metadata or information regarding the content of the page. If you possess a CMS sie that is originally produced by the web team of UMC tend to have pre-population of the data for you. However, it is considered crucial for you in reviewing and updating the Metadata as your site change with time.

Title Metadata:

It is responsible for the display fo page titles at the top part of the browser window and as the headline within the results of the search engine. It is considered as one of the most crucial metadata on the webpage. For those with the website of CMS, the development of the automated system by the website team for the creation of the Meta title for each page of the web on the basis of your page title. This adds to the importance of the use of the well-thought-out title of the page i.e. rich in keywords.

Description Metadata

The textual description used by the browser in your page search return is referred to as Description metadata. Consider it as the window display of your site i.e. appealing as well as a concise description of what it contains with the objective of providing encouragement to people to enter. A good meta description will mainly contain two complete sentences. Often, meta descriptions are not always used by the search engines but it is thought to give them the option.

Keyword Metadata

Keyword metadata is rare and is often used for tabulating the rankings of search engines. However, you must be aware of the keyword phrases which might not be thought to lead to any unnecessary damage to your keyword metadata. But, you must include a variety of keyword phrases. Considering the general rule, make your efforts in keeping it to about 3-7 keyword phrases which consist of 1-4 words.

Have a link-worthy site:

Focusing on the creation of the relevant links within the text. Despite to have click here links, trying to write out the destination name. Click here has no value of search engine beyond the attached URL whereas the Michigan Tech Enterprise Program involves lots of keywords and thus improves the ranking of the search engine as well as the page rankings that you are linked to. Therefore, you must use descriptive links through developing keywords linking. This not only brings improvement in search engine optimization but significantly adds value to your readers which includes those with disabilities or the ones who use screen readers.

Use alt tags:

The description of the visual and video media must be done through alt tags or the descriptions of alternative text. The use of alt tags significantly allows search engines for locating your page which is thought to be crucial particularly for those who use the screen readers or text-only browsers.

Do not be boring:

How do you say or convey your thoughts to your readers? Make sure to always use your own perspective, personal stories, case studies and even amusing anecdotes that significantly turn your post to be more interesting. You need to ask yourself why any of the readers would want to read your post. If you are unable to find the answer, you need to make your content more engaging or select another topic.

Do not be afraid of catchy headlines:

Trying to find out the attention-grabbing title is considered one of the finest ways of getting the eye of the busy surfer. You need to be creative, intriguing, exciting, and engaging. This might be the classic Top 10 tips or something just like this but finding this would be considered as much more challenging solution such as Why people can be bothered to read your blog post. It is okay to make your title different from the URL that can be more rick with keywords.

Do not write about what you do not know:

Credibility is considered to be a key factor of being a blogger so you do not need to make any kind of claims that you cannot provide support to or set yourself up as a professionalist in this particular domain that you do not know much about. To maxim, 'Write about what you are aware of as it upholds very true meaning in blogging.

Do not forget to include images:

One of my friends is a blogger and writes really great articles but he often uses photos or videos in order to provide support to his writing which significantly makes it less attractive or leads to dull read. Most of the successful bloggers use images for the illustration of the articles. You must make sure to use your own or take permission before using photos and do not forget to always credit the creator until and unless it is required.

Mistakes to avoid:

A great deal of hard work and attention is required to write good and quality content. You do not need to be extremely meticulous in each aspect of both the style and content to get the desired influence on your reader. Despite a careful approach, even an expert writer of the content can make mistakes. Quite often, bloggers commit a lot many mistakes which can make a blog fare in a poor manner regarding quality. Thus, below are the few visible and unavoidable mistakes in blogging:

Set Unrealistic Goals:

You are well aware of your abilities and schedules better than anyone else so do not make the habit of posting daily if you cannot do so. Start it with weekly posting and get in the groove. As soon as you get with the increase your posting if you can.

Breaking point your assertion check.

On the off chance, you have a remark, say it. Readers (and web crawlers) want to get meatier pieces (500 words or more) to make navigating worth their time. This doesn't mean you can't include shorter pieces or that you should chatter just to meet a word check, however, don't be reluctant to separate outdated discernments that websites should be short. At the point when everything looks good, go long.

Commit syntax errors.

Furthermore, in the event, you do, right them right away. People on the Web will, in general, be increasingly tolerant about grammatical mistakes, so don't worry about it on the off chance, you do commit an error. Be that as it may, right it when you can. Keep in mind, in the event, you ever need readers to pay attention to you, you need to take yourself (and your blog) genuinely. Give it the expert quality it merits.

Be negative.

It's commonly rash to air individual complaints openly (except if, obviously, that is the topic of your blog). You'll go significantly further by being certain, motivational and strong to the network that you're writing to.

Compose long paragraphs.

Long squares of content are difficult for readers to process, particularly when perusing on PCs and tablets. Separate your content into shorter passages, visual cues, and records at whatever point conceivable. Likewise, on the off chance, you can, work in certain subheads.

Abstain from attempting new things.

It's critical to let your blog advance after some time, and the main way this can happen is in the event, you go out on a limb each once in for a moment. Regardless of whether it's including infographics or individual stories or visitor bloggers, never be hesitant to take a stab at something new. In the event, you feel it can add something unique to your blog, attempt it.

Absence of data isolation

As the lack of segregation of data you have collected is considered to be a platform to edit your content, it is required by the content writers to make efforts to represent related points in your content in an appropriate manner to keep readers engaged. Similarly, the lack of appropriate formatting and presentation would lead to making any blog look lacking. So, it is important for you to make sure that your content blog is represented under the proper headline and sorted things. However, it is not rare to make errors while you start blogging, it is somehow completely dependent on you how you get started with it.

We as a whole commit blogging errors, even those of us who've been doing this for a considerable length of time. Be that as it may, with this manual for help point you the correct way towards keeping away from the absolute most exorbitant blogging botches, I will probably accelerate your advancement and stork your energy.

Email marketing and google analytics (how to track results and improve with data-driven analysis)

Email promoting is significant for creating a business. Being an extremely proficient and practical method for reinforcing client connections, making brand mindfulness and expanding deals, it has become a crucial device for each advertiser.

As an advertiser, you realize that it is so imperative to utilize information to fuel your showcasing efforts. Luckily for you, email showcasing instruments like Campaign Monitor coordinate straightforwardly with Google Analytics, so you can perceive what number of individuals are tapping on your email crusades, arriving on your site, and proceeding to become leads and clients.

Email advancing is noteworthy for delivering business. Being a capable and monetarily keen technique for sustaining customer associations, making brand care and extending gives, it has become an essential instrument for every sponsor. Regardless, how to measure and propel your email advancing endeavors remains noteworthy stress for most associations. The fitting reaction is really clear: You ought to use a free anyway overwhelming device called Google Analytics for email advancing estimation. There are various focal points of assessing email advancing through Google Analytics.

Google Analytics makes following the entirety of your promoting information simpler, and as a little something extra, it's not very hard to get set up. This article will exhibit a bit by bit showcasing information following methodology, with the goal that you can begin agonizing over the greater things.

Why use Google Analytics?

Potentially the most compelling motivation why you should utilize Google Analytics to follow showcasing information of yours is a straightforward reality that the device is free. It's an incredible asset that offers significant data you need so as to follow your advertising endeavors. This examination can give you bits of knowledge into what's really working and what zones may require improvement.

One key motivation behind why Google Analytics works so well is that as a Google program itself, it works successfully with other Google programs that are useful for your showcasing endeavors, similar to Search Console, YouTube, and AdWords.

Setting up Google Analytics:

At the point when you have set up Google Analytics for your site, you can follow the source your site guests are coming. On the off chance, you go above and beyond and set up an email battle following additionally with Google Analytics, further division of the email traffic is conceivable. This is conceivable when you make identifiable URLs by setting up UTM parameters. These UTM parameters or labels are little snippets of data that are included toward the finish of any connection that you remember for your messages. The means associated with setting this up are:

- Open a free Google Analytics to represent your site.

- Add Google Analytics following your site to associate it.

- To set up the following for email crusades, make your

identifiable URLs by setting up the UTM parameters.

You can likewise utilize it to overlook traffic from administrators and different clients, track query items pages and 404 pages.

Incorporate All Analytics Platforms

In the event, you need to join Google Analytics information with extra investigation instruments and stages to pick up experiences about your traffic, attempt Segment. The platform enables you to oversee information from more than 100 distinctive promoting, examination, engineer, showcasing, deals, backing, and client testing stages in a single spot. Essentially introduce one bit of following code on your site, and the remainder of the following codes from any platform you pick are overseen by Segment.

Visualize Google Analytics Data

It's conceivable to view and analyze information from numerous sites simultaneously in Google Analytics with a device like Cyfe. You can even utilize it to make dashboards with a definite perspective on your sites' continuous traffic, including clients, domain of clients, traffic sources and content they're as of now seeing.

Find out About Email Marketing Traffic

Need to interface your email promoting endeavors to the traffic in Google Analytics? Email showcasing stages, for example, MailChimp, GetResponse, Constant Contact, and Vertical Response enable you to follow traffic from joins in your messages to your email battles.

For instance, MailChimp lets you check one box to add UTM parameters to joins when you make an email crusade so you can see traffic from those connections inside Google Analytics.

Making UTM parameters for Email Campaign Tracking Using Google URL Builder

The initial step to following the accomplishment of your email crusade is setting up Campaign Tracking. At the point when individuals go to your site from different locales like Twitter and Facebook, it's simple for Google Analytics to know where they originated from and label the traffic properly (as "social traffic," for example). In any case, on account of email, in the event, you don't utilize these easily overlooked details called "UTM factors," traffic from your email crusades will be named "Direct."

Some of the little fundamental parameters of UTM factors you would be able to add depending on your connections in the email battle to let Google Analytics know from where the content is from.

How would it be if we take a glimpse at the ongoing Canvas i.e. the battle of an email just as an example? Similarly, how would it look like with or without any UTM factors? Do you just need to see all the additional parameters seized towards the end of the URL? These are factors that tell the Google Analytics where they are from.

In spite of the fact, these connections look insane, they're simpler to set up than you might suspect. You have two choices: You can either label every one of your connections physically or, in case you're a Campaign Monitor client, you can turn on programmed interface labeling.

Making Advanced Segments in Google Analytics

Propelled Segments are basically channels that enable you to see information in your reports from explicit guests, for example, guests from search or guests from email. On the off chance, you set up an email battle following along these lines or by means of your ESP I prescribe you make a uniquely Advanced fragment where you disconnect guests from email (or various kinds of email) so you can see how they carry on and convert.

The Advanced fragment ought to be founded on all visits to the site with a vehicle of 'email' set, gave this is the means by which you have marked your connections by labeling them. The following domain tells you the best way to label your connections utilizing the battle following in Google Analytics.

To include a propelled fragment for Email advertising in Google Analytics, you should choose the propelled portion alternative utilizing the down bolt at the upper left over the reports in Google Analytics, at that point pick "Make New Segment" and set the medium to "Email".

Presently, you will have the option to see your email guests alongside your typical measurements. With everything set up in Google Analytics for email showcasing, how about we audit the reports.

Link Social and Website Engagement

In the event, you utilize online networking the executives' apparatuses like Buffer, Hootsuite, and Oktopost to distribute and plan updates to your top web-based life systems, you'll profit by connecting them to Google Analytics.

With Buffer, you can modify the UTM parameters you use to follow custom crusades inside Google Analytics so they coordinate the updates you distribute through Buffer. This alternative is remembered for the Buffer for field-tested strategies beginning at $50 every month.

Investigating Google Analytics' Powerful Reports

Since you have empowered Campaign Tracking and have set up email traffic as an Advanced Segment, you can take a gander at for all intents and purposes any report in Google Analytics and see the impact your email showcasing efforts have on the numbers.

To kick you off, here are four of our preferred reports for understanding the impact of your email promoting efforts:

The Overview Report:

Simply need to perceive what amount of traffic is your email showcasing endeavors are bringing to your site and contrast that within general rush hour gridlock? The outline report is the one for you.

To get to it, ensure you have your "Crusade Medium: Email" propelled section turned on, at that point basically select "Audience" from the left side menu and pick "Diagram."

The Campaign report

On the off chance, you need to see the real impact of every one of your battles and look at them against one another, at that point the Campaign Report is the place you need to be.

Ensure you have your "Crusade Medium: Email" propelled portion turned on and explore to "Procurement" in the left menu bar. At that point select "Crusades." Next, you'll need to choose the "Battle" connect simply over the table to sort the table by the most noteworthy performing efforts.

The Behavior Flow report

Have you at any point needed to realize what individuals do on your site once they land from your email battle? Do they simply leave? Or on the other hand, do they see your Pricing or Contact Us pages?

Luckily, the conduct stream report can let you know precisely what individuals do when they land at your site from a specific crusade.

To get to it, select "Conduct" from the left-hand menu and afterward select "Conduct Flow." Next, you'll have to choose "Crusades" from the little green drop-down menu over the principal segment in the report. This will give all of you your crusades, and, in the event, you need to see one specific battle, simply click it and pick "View just this portion."

See whether Google Updates Affect Your Website

Include the Fruition Google Penalty Checker to examine the information from your Google Analytics account and decide whether your site has been influenced decidedly or contrarily by Google refreshes.

Find Your (Not Provided) Keywords

For internet searcher advertisers, the loss of catchphrase information in Google Analytics was a disaster. Different devices like AuthorityLabs are attempting to recover that information once more.

You can utilize this information to make or upgrade points of arrival and site content to all the more likely focus for new catchphrases.

Link Ecommerce Sales Data

Internet business stages, for example, Shopify, Magento, and Bigcommerce offer nitty-gritty directions on the most proficient method to incorporate with Google Analytics to get experiences from the online business following reports.

These reports can assist you with learning a great deal about your web-based business income, from which items create the most income to the top traffic sources that send guests who eventually buy your items.

Data-Driven Marketing:

Data-driven email promoting is tied in with translating your information to all the more likely to comprehend your possibilities and clients. It likewise includes actualizing an email showcasing plan with the data and bits of knowledge you assemble to convey significant email battles that focus on every client's needs, inclinations, and interests.

With regards to taking your email battle results to the following level with the assistance of an information-driven advertising procedure, there are a few email measurements that are essential:

Email Campaign Performance

How fruitful are your email battles? Realizing the following measurements will give you a smart thought:

- Number of messages sent

- Number of opens and open rate

- Number of snaps and active clicking factor

- Click-to-open rate

- Number of withdraws and withdraw rate

- Number of skips and ricochet rate

- Spam objections and spam protest rate.

Inbox Deliverability

Is it accurate to say that you are having issues traversing the Internet specialist organizations' spam channels and into the inboxes of your supporters? It's critical to remain over the following measurements to recognize and rapidly manage any email deliverability gives that emerge:

- Number of messages sent by the domain

- Number of extraordinary opens by domain

- Number of skips by domain

- Number of squares by domain

- Number of withdraws by domain

- A number of spam protests by domain.

Conversion and ROI

Changes are the genuine proportion of an email crusade's prosperity. Contingent upon the objectives of your email-advertising program, coming up next are the kinds of the transformation measurements that you ought to follow:

- Conversion rate (the level of endorsers that tapped on a connection and finished the ideal activity, for example, making a buy)

- Number of offers by sort of email battle

- Total number of offers by month

- Overall ROI (complete income from your email battles isolated by the all outspend).

Some significant measurements that should shape some portion of all things considered, independent of your objectives, are given beneath.

Click-through rate (CTR) – This indicates the level of individuals who tapped on at any rate one connection in an email. Through this, you can without much of a stretch figure the presentation of each email sent and how CTR changes after some time.

Transformation Rate – This is the level of beneficiaries who tapped on, in any event, one connection inside an email and finished the source of inspiration like rounding out a structure or downloading a free digital book.

Bounce Rate – This rate signifies the messages that couldn't be effectively conveyed to the email addresses.

Rundown Growth Rate – This essentially implies the rate at which your email list is expanding. A solid development rate implies your compass and audience is growing.

Sending and Sharing Emails – The level of beneficiaries who shared the messages to any social platform by tapping on the sharing catches or sent to associates through the 'forward to a companion' button.

Return on investment (ROI) – You ought to have the option to figure the ROI of your email crusades.

Since you realize how to follow the entirety of your promoting information all the way, you're en route to simple improvements and higher ROI! In the event, you need some unimaginable revealing highlights at no cost, at that point go for Google Analytics to follow the measurements of your email promoting efforts. This productive revealing will help you in email advancement and expanding your ROI.

How To Generate Traffic

You've been buckling down on your blog, you feel set up. Presently it's an ideal opportunity to quit fooling around about traffic. It happens to potentially anyone. Sooner or later, every blogger faces a similar issue. It's the most despicable aspect of our reality. Some include minor changes to your content; others require a progressively crucial take a glimpse at how you approach blogging.

As indicated, advertisers who organize blogging are multiple times bound to see a positive quantifiable profit. In any case, you definitely know blogging is significant, which is the reason you as of now have one.

In this way, on the off chance, you compose well and are blogging about a subject where there is a sizeable intrigue, you can wind up with a lot of traffic on your site. What's more, we as a whole recognize what bunches of traffic to a site implies: expanded deals openings and income.

On the off chance, you need solid and qualified inquiry traffic however don't have a clue where to start, this post will be your best asset. Read it strictly and follow up on the pearls that you find.

It is nothing but a difficult task to be disappointed and abandon blogging, but once you will get started experiencing the benefits of it you will surely understand that your blog can tremendously influence your business through pulling in the peak hours gridlock to the page of your website. This will assists you in fabricating online networking traffic and establish a connection between probabilities and possibilities.

You truly care about your audience.

Be that as it may, in some cases, regardless of getting everything done right, the traffic's a flop.

That is the point at which the inquiries start – am I sufficient? Well, does blogging even work as an authentic plan of action? Am I burning through my time?

In the event, that is you, let me dispel any confusion air by citing Jon Morrow, "All of us chooses what our identity is. No, you may not be prepared to be a well-known blogger now, however you can get prepared."

Blogging works. We've seen a ton of verification around us for that. The issue isn't blogging; it is doing things that don't yield trust or traffic to your blog.

10 years back you could wrench out a 300-word piece and get progressively content distributed, left, right and focus. Back then, simply having something distributed implied you could pull in immense rush hour gridlock. Since very few were doing it.

For what reason do you need more traffic?

Things being what they are, you have a blog, yet need more traffic?

To start with, check your intentions: Is it help individuals, be an asset, and have any kind of effect? Or on the other hand to put you on the map?

In the event, the last mentioned, quit blogging now. On the off chance, you're blogging for self-serving reasons, at that point that might be the genuine inhibitor to your blog's development. Since here's the reality:

Individuals need you to discuss them, not you.

It's alright to expound on close to home encounters and offer what you've gained from a direct viewpoint, yet be cautious about making yourself into some sort of blog demigod. Rather, mean to be an asset and help to other people.

The incongruity is that in the event, you do that, you'll wind up turning into a star.

So on the off chance, you need more traffic to your blog, don't concentrate on the traffic. Concentrate on the individuals.

The following are demonstrated ways that can assist you with boosting readership and increase traffic to your blog.

Find Your Way:

Before starting to write your quality content, it is considered important for the investment of the little understanding of the energy of your intended interest group and what you find out what do they search for.

You can rapidly fabricate a group of people structure by responding to the following inquiries:

- Who is your intended interest group?

- What issues would they say they are confronting that you can help illuminate?

- What sort of content would they say they are searching for?

- How might they in a perfect world attempt to discover the solutions to their inquiries?

Addressing these inquiries will assist you with getting a more clear image of your intended interest group.

You can likewise develop this by including additionally customized inquiries, for example,

- How old would they say they are?

- What are their occupations?

- What is their training level?

- What is their mastery level in the topic of your blog?

These audience profiles are otherwise called purchaser personas in the eCommerce business. On the off chance, you run an online store, at that point, we strongly prescribe that you look at this itemized guide on the most proficient method to make a purchaser persona with models and layouts.

Locate the correct author! (Clue: that probably won't be you)

At the core of getting your blog saw, and driving loads of traffic to it is composing extremely incredible content – and that content will be greatly improved if the individual composing it is both proficient and enthusiastic about what they are expounding on.

Posts that are composed of the heart – and not by a content ranch – are unmistakably bound to be the posts that intrigue individuals and vitally, get shared.

In any case, the reality of the situation might prove that you actually are not the best individual to compose the posts for your site. Maybe you're not an incredible author; maybe you don't have the opportunity to give to blogging.

In the event, both of those announcements seem like it may concern you, consider finding an essayist who is equipped for making extremely incredible posts and placing in the hours to do as such.

Whoever winds up composing the posts on your site, their character needs to radiate through. Readers relate to journalists in light of the fact, there is a lot to like (or even abhorrence) about their character, bombastic character or manner of speaking.

On the off chance, a readr likes YOU as an essayist – and not simply the nature of the content you are delivering – you are unmistakably bound to draw in a devoted after.

Thus, ensure your character runs over in your posts; this encourages you to structure an affinity with your readers, who might be increasingly disposed of therefore to return to your blog essentially on the grounds that they like you as a person.

Website design enhancement Wordpress Plugins for Bloggers

There are some extraordinary WordPress plugins intended to assist bloggers with SEO. They make it simple to set up your URL slugs accurately, assist you with creating flawless meta depictions, arrangement sitemaps, and help you in exploring other SEO specialized bits that may not fall into place for bloggers.

Two top picks are:

- Wordpress SEO by Yoast

- Across the board SEO Pack

Finding Long Tail Keywords

Considering Search Engine Optimization, keywords are at the core of SEO. Possibly some of the most uncomplicated approaches for the production of more traffic to your site in order to guarantee that every page on your webpage has a keyword procedure. So for the composition of each blog you need to select one key expression that you need to accept readers would significantly use in finding that post.

Next, the incorporation of the keyword phrase into the post title, the headline on the page, within the content for an approximate of two times in a featured image on the page and the part of the page link. The concentration on the keyword assists in the understanding of Google what the page is all about, which tends to lead to increased traffic from the search engines.

Make a Newsletter To Showcase Your Best Blog Posts

Advancement should be a major piece of your content technique, with the goal that your well-deserved blog entries drive that traffic you so frantically want!

One snappy and simple approach to begin driving more traffic to your blog is to begin gathering messages for a blog pamphlet. When you've caught those gets in touch with, you can send them week by week or month to month messages including your best posts, taking effectively commonplace guests directly back to your site. Since these clients are as of now OK with your blog, odds are they may investigate more on their following visit. Who knows what they'll discover?

Making Kickass Headlines

At the point when clients locate your content in list items or RSS channels, the main thing they see is your article feature.

An appealing blog entry title sticks out and gets more snaps. Though a plain and exhausting feature gets disregarded, and clients are probably going to look by it.

This stands out as truly newsworthy significant.

You have to figure out how to compose better titles for your blog entries that catch client consideration and get more snaps.

Fortunately, blogging specialists have been doing research on features for quite a while, and you can profit by their discoveries.

These are the fundamental structure squares of a viable feature:

A decent feature triggers a passionate reaction (delight, shock, stun, interest, dread, fervor, ravenousness, etc).

It offers clients a prize and worth

It advances the content by including objective watchwords

Marketing specialists use control words to trigger enthusiastic reactions. They explain to clients why the article is important or what they will get from tapping on the feature.

Finally, a great feature incorporates a source of inspiration for clients which is regularly unobtrusive and here and there suggested.

To find out additional, we prescribe you to look at these features that turned into a web sensation and what you can gain from them.

You can likewise utilize the following free feature analyzer devices to help make better features:

- CoSchedule Headline Analyzer

- ShareThrough Headline Analyzer

- EMV Headline Analyzer

Our group normally utilizes these three devices to make better blog entry titles and features.

As a blogger, you ought to consistently guarantee that you're making compellingly great features. Your feature is the thing that gets guests to your site and catches their advantage.

Some even recommend that your feature is a higher priority than your genuine post! On the off chance, you have an extraordinary content piece taking cover behind a ratty feature, it'll kick the bucket a snappy passing. Appearances are everything, and similarly, as you wouldn't appear at a wedding wearing your remain at home-wiped out garments, you can't depend on dreary features to advance your blog entries.

Try not to be reluctant to try different things with various features. Offer your post on various occasions with various features and see which style works best.

Plugins, Integrations, And Omnichannel Strategy

Plugins, as we as a whole know, expand WordPress' abilities. It is nothing unexpected that the blogging business has been developing quickly since the early advancement of the web. As indicated by WordPress, 409 million individuals see in excess of 20 billion blog entries every month starting today. This shows individuals' enthusiasm for online journals has been expanding just as its requests.

To begin with a blogging site, numerous individuals discover WordPress as an advantageous source. You can without much of a stretch make a WordPress site by following some straightforward strides for blogging. Other than sites, individuals do will, in general, make WordPress sites for business, news, magazines, and portfolios as well.

There are a huge number of free and premium WordPress plugins out there. It very well may be overpowering to locate the best plugins among those decisions! What's more, when you're simply beginning a blog, you probably won't recognize what plugins to search for.

Which Plugins Should You Use?

With regards to plugins, how would you pick which to add to your blog?

To think of this rundown, I approached my Facebook fans for proposals.

Mainstream plugins fall into several classifications: those that upgrade your readers' understanding, and those in the background that help you with blog the board and enhancement.

Plugins

The creation of a blog about any particular topic by the user but having a successful blog is related to the plugins on the blog. The WordPress plugins mainly involve security, search engine optimization, admin, visuals, themes and much more. The plugins in the list are high-rated, high quality, completely affordable and highly customizable.

1. Yoast SEO

If you have intended to start a blog, you cannot go much far without any good search engine optimization. Yoast SEO is considered as one of the most utilized and best plugins for blogs in regards to the search engine optimization. It has significantly been trusted by the owners of the WordPress Websites which is frequently being used by updating the better upgrades and be compatible with the algorithms of Google. Because of this reason, it is mainly regarded as the number one plugin in SEO. Yoast has a great deal of highlights that can make your blog viably better. It can enhance your watchwords and equivalent words. It likewise breaks down the lucidness of your blog and figures the Flesch Reading Ease score. Other than this, it can likewise enhance the pictures that you can post in your blog so your online journals can be positioned higher with the assistance of the catchphrases in the picture titles and traits as well.

2. Editorial Calendar

When Courtney and I were getting into the furrow of presenting on the Buffer blog, we thought that it was useful to remain sorted out with an article schedule. The Editorial Calendar WordPress module appeared to do the stunt fine and dandy. It snatched the entirety of our planned posts and drafts, and it put them on a conveniently sorted out schedule so we could see initially what content was coming up.

Maybe my preferred component of the module was the cool way you could move various stories around the schedule, and it would refresh the schedule as well as the post itself. It was tremendous assistance for keeping all our content sorted out and our group in a state of harmony.

3. Akismet

Akismet is an authority WordPress module from Automattic to avoid spam remarks in WordPress. Created by Matt Mullenweg and Automattic (the individuals behind WordPress.com), Akismet investigations your remarks, at that point obstructs the spam. It's free for non-business locales.

It is the first module that you ought to introduce on any new blog. Your new blog will have the WordPress remarking highlight, and in the event, you don't utilize this module, your blog will be spammed. The spammers just need to toss their connections on your articles and would prefer not to join the exchange.

This module will consequently move those remarks that it considers spam into the waste can (erasing them for all time after a timeframe).

4. WP-Optimize

As a blogger, you'll most likely spare a post commonly before hitting distribute, correct? I regularly spare my posts around nine or multiple times, so I know how these things go. Be that as it may, did you realize that these post modifications are buried in the WordPress database? These are amendments you are never under any circumstance going to require again, so why keep them? Answer: don't!

WP-Optimize is one of the fundamental plugins for bloggers. It totally cleans up your WordPress database of draft post updates, just as a large number of spam remarks that collect. For what reason is this significant? Since it can make your site load quicker.

5. UpdraftPlus

UpdraftPlus is a famous WordPress reinforcement module. Before you make any significant move on your blog like changing a subject, refreshing a module, or update WordPress center, it is prescribed to make a total reinforcement. In the case of anything turns out badly, you can reestablish the reinforcement utilizing UpdraftPlus immediately.

Regardless of how solid your WordPress facilitating is or how cautious you are, there's constantly an opportunity something can turn out badly. In the event, the most exceedingly awful occurs and you get hacked or your site goes down, you need to be readied. Updraft makes it simple to in a split second reestablish your site, in the event, something goes wrong.

6. Grammarly

Grammarly is a straightforward program augmentation that works incredibly with a WordPress blog. It enables you to improve your content by evading little linguistic and spelling botches that you could miss accidentally while composing blog entries.

As a blogger, you wear a ton of caps – creator, author, editorial manager, editor, distributor, and the sky is the limit from there! It's hard to discover each and every spelling and sentence structure botch when everything relies upon only you.

That is the reason it's savvy to utilize an apparatus like Grammarly to twofold check your work. Leaving those errors on your blog can give an amateurish impression to your readers and hurt your image.

7. WP Rocket

Your site's speed will represent the moment of truth your SEO endeavors and significantly affect change rates, as well. Subsequently, accelerating WordPress is something you should pay attention to.

With regards to WordPress speed, few plugins can contend with WP Rocket. Certainly, the $39 sticker price may put off specialists, however, this across the board module is ensured to thump seconds off your heap time.

It ships with all the speed-improving usefulness you might want, including page and program storing, GZIP pressure, minification, apathetic stacking, and CDN.

One of the most significant plugins for bloggers and some other WordPress clients!

8. MonsterInsights:

One of the best modules of Google Analytics is the MonsterInsight for WordPress. It significantly enables you with the appropriate interface of the website with Google Analytics allowing you for precise searching and utilization of the website.

It significantly provides you with all the required details regarding the issues directly in the dashboard of WordPress.

You can then go for the optimization of the website in order to increase the traffic of your website, subscribers and generation of revenue. We have been provided with detailed guidelines regarding the installation of Google Analytics in

WordPress, how to use Google Analytics for enabling the tracking of eCommerce and how to track the engagement of the user.

It is present with free versions but it is only known for unlocking while the upgrade of the Pro-version. Additionally, in order to get a 50 percent discount, you can surely use MonsterInsights coupons for purchase.

9. Sucuri

Security needs to considered as one of the first priority for all the owners of the online business. It offers a security Plugin of WordPress and a web application firewall and is thought to be one of the best ways of providing protection you can potentially get for your site.

It deals with monitoring and protection of your website from DDoS, threats of malware, brute force attacks and some other kinds of attacks. If you do not uphold a firewall on your website then you are required to add one right today.

You can improve your skills by strengthening your website security in order to provide protection to your business. Sucuri assists in blocking hundreds and thousands of attacks each month on WPBeginneer.

10. Woocommerce

WooCommerce is the most mainstream eCommerce module for WordPress utilized by more than 4 million sites.

It accompanies all the ground-breaking highlights that you have to make an online store.

In the course of the most recent couple of years, WooCommerce has set up itself as the most prevailing eCommerce module for WordPress. There's even a WooCommerce biological system now with committed

WooCommerce facilitating, WooCommerce topics, and WooCommerce plugins accessible.

The extraordinary news about these WordPress web-based business modules is that they give indistinguishable highlights and advantages from SaaS items, and you get amazing help assets, flourishing improvement networks, and incorporation with the least demanding content the board framework on the planet. You'll likewise get a few expansions and remarkable incorporations for things like email advertising and installment entryways.

Omni-Channel Strategy:

Omnichannel is characterized as a multi-channel deals approach that furnishes the client with incorporated client experience. The client can be shopping on the web from a work domain or cell phone, or by phone, or in a physical store and the experience would be consistent.

It's significant here to recognize an omnichannel experience from a multi-channel understanding. Basically, it comes down to the profundity of the coordination.

You can have stunning versatile promoting, drawing in online networking efforts, and a well-structured site. In any case, on the off chance, they don't cooperate, it's not omnichannel.

The multi-channel experience is the thing that most organizations put resources into today. They have a site, blog, Facebook, and Twitter. They utilize every one of these stages to draw in and associate with clients. Be that as it may, much of the time, the client still comes up short on a consistent encounter and predictable informing over every one of these channels.

The five hints underneath could give you a head start.

1. Optimize your hierarchical structure

Your clients hold little respect for the inside structure of your business, and which is all well and good. At whatever point a client collaborates with an organization they consider it a solitary, brought together brand, not an assortment of different offices and information sources.

To convey the consistent experience that clients expect, you have to impart your items and administrations in a predictable manner, and that consistency starts at home.

Your initial step is to get all your association's specialties energetic about your new vision. Omnichannel promoting is accomplished through inside cooperation and requires incorporated groups and advances. You need every one of your domains of expertise to be in agreement, advancing a similar brand, a similar message and at last, putting the client as a matter of first importance.

You'll likewise need to have the correct individuals in the ideal spot at the opportune time. When you set up omnichannel advertising, you will recognize various touch focuses where clients may interface with your association and spots that may influence their basic leadership and want to buy your items or administrations.

2. Integrate your investigation

You could begin by mapping your present information catch framework. At that point set up another announcing structure and guarantee every region records information in a similar degree of detail, progressively and in a way that is anything but difficult to dissect. Store the data in a focal spot. When setting up, you can incorporate offsite information, for example, deals information and stock keeping. This will give you a superior perspective on all the various manners by which your clients collaborate with you.

A case of advanced business tasks can be found in Alibaba's 'new retail' model, which incorporates physical stores with web-based shopping, and coordinations frameworks with interchanges. The outcome is an intelligent shopping experience for clients and a precise perspective on stock crosswise over stores and the web for the retailer.

3. Become client-driven

Understanding your clients better and adding profundity to your association with them will assist you in recognizing the most productive client gatherings. You'll be responsive, straightforward and interface with them in manners that they start, and your investigation will assume a key job in this.

Correspondences content ought to be custom-made to suit the individual conduct of a client. Draw a guide or schedule of the customer venture and the choice focuses along that voyage. Make content to suit the diverse navigational choices the client could make, contemplating socioeconomics and characters and analyzing smaller scale fragments through your examination.

4. Synchronize your channels

A definitive objective is to accomplish cooperative energy between each channel and to do that you need a commitment procedure that gives reliable informing overall client contact focuses just as the innovation that connections various gadgets –, for example, cell phone, application, tablet, workstation, and PCs.

A thing put in a shopping basket on a home PC ought to likewise appear on the client's telephone application. Or then again a rebate offered online should, in any case, be accessible to the client on the off chance, they stroll into the physical store.

Connecting innovation, interchanges, and gadgets will assist you with monitoring your clients just as giving a consistent client experience. Your investigation will figure out where and how clients discover data, which gadgets they like and when they are well on the way to purchase items and administrations.

5. Move clients closer to your image

With this action and a huge number of potential outcomes, you'll need an overall and firm advertising methodology that draws clients nearer to your image and creates benefits.

Your methodology ought to give a strong system to adjusted advertising exercises and decide your objectives and targets over different channels all in all.

At the point when you compose your technique, foresee that purchasers may begin in one channel and move to another. This change must be consistent. Ensure your system provides group guidance on the most proficient method to react to client associations and how to give them a decent brand experience paying little mind to their choices.

Omnichannel advertising isn't a strategy.

It's not by any means a tip or a pattern. It's an advancement.

It's the meeting up of a wide range of variables (like versatile and social) to propel the manner in which purchasers hope to shop.

However, omnichannel showcasing isn't really simple to execute, either. It requires expanded coordination and streamlining of administrations.

That additional work, however, at last, pays off. It gives a superior encounter to customers.

Also, the best part is that more open doors for development for retailers.

Organizations are never again bound to simply retail or choked to open and close occasions of their physical domains.

Copywriting: Do It Yourself Or Outsource It

Copywriting is the craftsmanship and study of composing duplicate (words utilized on-site pages, advertisements, special materials, and so on.) that sells your item or administration and persuades forthcoming clients to make a move. From various perspectives, it resembles employing one sales rep to arrive at all of your clients. A business group contacts clients each in turn; a publicist arrives at all of them without a moment's delay through announcements, magazine promotions, direct mail advertisements, blog entries, and that's only the tip of the iceberg.

Configuration, content advertising, SEO, and development hacking are large parts of a total advanced showcasing plan, however, copywriting is the paste that ties everything together. Duplicate gives your structure importance and establishes the framework for your content showcasing, SEO, and development hacking. Composing a better duplicate empowers you to change over more readers into clients, and we needed to give a guide that would give you a bit of leeway when composing duplicate both on and disconnected.

On the off chance, you can use your composition to recount a convincing story while persuading clients regarding the requirement for your item, there is no restriction on the development your business can understand.

Do it without anyone's help:

Endeavor your opposition's shortcomings.

To compose a convincing duplicate, it is fundamental that you realize what separates your item from the challenge. When you know your rivals' shortcomings, you should ensure your audience knows them and comprehends why purchasing your rivals' items would be a horrendous misstep.

Begin by altogether inquiring about your opposition and understanding what they offer as far as items and administrations. Next, list the components of their contributions that are sub-par compared to your own. Don't hesitate to destroy the challenge however be reasonable in your examinations. You need to have the option to help your cases on the off chance, you are tested.

Know your audience:

Each individual on the planet won't see each advertisement on the planet. Every advertisement has a particular audience that will see it, and it's the advertiser's business to locate the best position to guarantee the intended interest group will see it. For instance, an advertisement for skateboards set in a nearby senior resident lodging affiliation bulletin isn't probably going to create a ton of offers. Truth be told, it would be a misuse of publicizing dollars.

The intended interest group for skateboards is adolescents or youthful grown-ups. Most by far of senior residents don't utilize skateboards, and it's anything but an item classification wherein they normally buy blessings. Before you purchase the advertisement domain, profit in the correct spot to get the greatest value for your money as far as introduction and building attention to your item or administration.

To start with, set aside the effort to examine your clients completely. In many organizations, 20 percent of clients are liable for 80 percent of offers (this is known as the 80/20 principle in the event, you're interested in the official showcasing wording for this wonder).

That 20 percent speaks to your best client, and your responsibility is to figure out who that 20 percent is. Assess your clients and set up together a statistic profile of your most important client, so you can publicize in the best places to discover comparative individuals who are likely prospects.

There are numerous credits you can use to build up a statistic profile of your clients. Following is a rundown of instances of characteristics to assist you with beginning your own statistic profiling activity:

- Gender

- Age

- Ethnicity

- Family Status

- Income

- Occupation

- Interests

Concentrate on "you," not "we."

It is fundamental that you know about how you're tending to your clients in your duplicate. To do this, you have to comprehend pronoun utilization. Recollect your school days. Recollect your English educator clarifying first individual, second individual, and third individual? As a boost, first individual (I, me, my, mine, we, us, our, our own) is the individual talking and second individual (you, your, yours) is the individual to whom one is talking.

It's fundamental that you compose duplicate that addresses your intended interest group and not at them- - and not about you. In this manner, most of your duplicate in any promotion or advertising piece ought to be written in the subsequent individual.

For instance, do you lean toward duplicate that says, "Through our top-notch deals office, we can convey autos inside 24 hours" or "You can drive your new vehicle tomorrow"? While the primary duplicate model spotlights on the business, the subsequent model spotlights on clients and talks legitimately to them. It's progressively close to home, and therefore, increasingly powerful.

Keep in mind, writing in the subsequent individual helps your audience rapidly associate the focuses in your duplicate to their own lives and enables them to customize the ad or advertising piece. This is the means by which the advertisement is associated with an individual client's very own life. By composing your duplicate so it centers around the client as opposed to yourself, the client can customize the promotion and item you're selling and act as needs are.

Maintain a strategic distance from T.M.I. (Too Much Information)

Never hazard losing the consideration of your audience by giving an excessive amount of detail in your duplicate. Successful copywriting mentions to your audience what they have to know to act and make a buy or how to get in touch with you for more data. Unessential subtleties mess the brains of your audience, which expands the probability of them overlooking the most significant parts of your commercial or showcasing program.

Except if you're promoting a professionally prescribed medication, profoundly specialized gear, or an exceedingly directed or confused item, the best rule to pursue is K.I.S.S. (Keep It Simple, Stupid). You're spending a generous measure of your promoting spending plan on putting every advertisement. With every advertisement, you just get a modest quantity of room to communicate as the need should arise to your audience. Astutely utilize that expensive land to guarantee you get the best yield on your speculation.

Incorporate a source of inspiration.

The objective of any promotion or advertising piece is to evoke some sort of reaction from the audience who sees it. A source of inspiration is the component of a duplicate that tells a group of people how you need them to react to your promotion or showcasing piece. Regularly, the source of inspiration makes a desire to move quickly around a message and gives directions on what to do straight away. For instance, a source of inspiration may advise the audience to consider the promoter or visit their store or site.

Counting a source of inspiration is by a long shot the most significant part of successful copywriting. It is basic that you make it simple for your audience to follow up on your promotion or showcasing message. You previously convinced them to need your item by finishing Step 1 Step 7 of the copywriting diagram and by composing a compelling duplicate. Presently you should ensure your audience can react effectively to your promotion and purchase your item by convincing them to act.

Edit.

It is important that you precisely edit your duplicate. Probably the snappiest approach to lose believability in promoting is to enable syntactic or spelling blunders to show up in your ad or advertising pieces. Clients make an interpretation of the lack of regard in promotions into thoughtlessness in items and administration. They ask themselves, "If this organization couldn't care less enough to create an advertisement without blunders, how likely are they to think about dealing with me?"

Professional organizations produce proficient quality promotions and promotion duplicate, and that implies their duplicate has been edited over and over and is sans mistake. Where to find people to outsource tasks.

Outsourcing:

For what reason Should You Outsource Your Blog Writing?

The greatest downside of content creation is that now is the right time expending. Today, 10% of advertisers go through between 16-20 hours every week on their web-based social networking content alone. At the point when you grow that to blog composing, article production, and realistic creation, it becomes evident exactly the amount of a weight making extraordinary content can be for occupied supervisors and entrepreneurs.

For some organizations, this weight is simply excessively. Lamentably, content is additionally too important to even think about ignoring. Organizations that put resources into content remain to appreciate the following advantages:

- A greater audience

- Set up power

- An affinity and commitment with watchers

- Chances to transform leads into clients

- The capacity to recount to your story

- A platform to meet new individuals

- The capacity to stick out

- Ability to mark yourself as a specialist in your industry

- The chance to profit and expand the organization's main concern

Absence of time – great content requires some serious energy. Regardless of whether you have a talented advertising group, they might not have the opportunity to deal with everything themselves. This can prompt other significant promoting errands missing cutoff times or going fixed.

Absence of ability/assets – if your business lacks profound pockets to put resources into an in-house group, or your showcasing group is little, you might not have the assets and aptitudes to fabricate your system and produce high-caliber, significant content.

Expanded/overpowering requests on in-house showcasing staff – putting your expanding content requests on your current staff can prompt decreasing quality and resolve, and conceivably wear out.

Absence of versatility – you can't just contract staff when content prerequisites are high, and afterward, let them go when you have to move back on content generation.

Organizations who are Outsourcing blog composing have more opportunities to take a shot at the business as opposed to in the business. Truth be told, proficient blog composing can work to improve all these fundamental advantages.

When Should you Outsource?

there are some other valid justifications to Outsourcing content creation:

You're excessively occupied. Discovering time to make content io inconceivable.

You loathe composing. Each time you plunk down to compose a post, you feel physically wiped out. Hemingway's statement, "There's nothing to composing. Everything you do is to sit at a and drain" reverberates profoundly with you.

You're in an industry that requires domain ability. You need a topic master to make articles and give precise counsel.

You have a spending limit. You're as of now doing content advertising and can see the ROI. You should simply twofold down and scale it up.

Advantages:

Outsourcing Passes Content Creation Along To Professionals

On the off chance, you don't work in content creation, you'll wind up at a checked hindrance. Experts who work in the content business know each niche and crevice, shrouded detail, and pattern. They see each sort of content, and they work to best use it for their customers. This enables you to make better content in all cases.

Outsourcing Content = Quality Content

At the point when you work with an Outsourcing content creation group, you get a group of experts that incorporates editors and essayists. This guarantees quality.

Each bit of content you outsourcing gets a thorough survey before it goes live. This averts spelling and sentence structure botches and guarantees that all your content is material your image is glad to append its name to.

Hands-Off Ease

Ever needed to make a circumstance where you don't need to consider your content by any means? Outsourcing your blog composing can get it going.

Content creation groups can make, oversee, and post all your content for you, enabling you to kick back and appreciate the ride, without the issue and weight of dealing with a group.

Lower Costs

Organizations contemplating staffing an in-house content curation group need to think about the expense. It's not just a question of finding and procuring qualified colleagues. This number likewise incorporates finding the domain, devices, and spending plan for the whole office.

Outsourcing enables you to diminish your overhead and spotlight on what is important the most: skilled, proficient help.

Productivity

As an entrepreneur, you can't do everything. The sooner you acknowledge this reality, the better. You're not superhuman. Nobody can do everything, and nobody group can like to deal with each feature of your business—that is the reason Outsourcing is developing: it's appointment without the extra overhead.

Time Savings

In-house content creation and advancement requires some serious energy. What's more, let's be honest; it takes money, as well! You're paying your in-house workers (in any event, we trust you are). It's presumable it is possible that you're increasing their compensation to cover the new remaining task at hand, or you're over-burdening them at a similar compensation rate.

In any case, you're abhorring greatest efficiency. Outsourcing enables the chance to make a hearty, versatile, beneficial content advancement machine for your business.

More grounded Content

Banding together with a content advancement organization, content promoting firm, or copywriting office gives you quick access to aptitude, specialization (did you realize you can employ master content makers, who can expound on money-related, lawful, medicinal, and other expert themes?) and capability it very well may be troublesome or difficult to make in-house. This furnishes your image with a lot more grounded content, directly off the bat.

Plan For Success With Your Outsourced Content Team

Content is basic for every incredible business today. Notwithstanding building up your skill, it likewise opens your organization to potential purchasers and drives potential clients to act.

All things considered, it's too imperative to even think about letting it fall by the wayside. At the point when you Outsourcing your blog composing, you outfit yourself with a solid, proficient group that is available to you no matter what. A savvy utilization of your assets and time, Outsourcing content creation is a utilitarian business move that can set you up for an eventual fate of achievement.

Keep up Your Enthusiasm.

Outsourcing one of a kind content creation causes you to remain amped up for your business and items. Exploring and composing the content, deciding the best sorts of content to utilize, choosing when and how to utilize content promoting, and different assignments rapidly channel your excitement. What's more, it's difficult to compose the energetic content your clients need when you get a handle on consumed.

By Outsourcing a few or the entirety of your content creation needs, you can keep your energy and eagerness about your organization and monitor your vitality for different tasks. Simultaneously, the composing organization's authors infuse that equivalent energy and fervor into the content they make for you, so both you and your clients can be amped up for what you do.

Increase A Trusted Content Marketing Partner.

Outsourcing to the correct organization makes a solid, trustworthy relationship you can use to make and advance more and better remarkable content. By becoming more acquainted with your business and industry, your content creation firm can compose all the more successfully and morally and with an elevated level of value and energy. The office turns into the accomplice you trust to assist you with benefiting as much as possible from your content.

At the point when your Outsourcing composing group turns into a confided in expansion of your in-house group, you have more than expanded limit. You have individuals you can depend on to take care of business well and on schedule, who go well beyond your desires, and who truly need to enable you to succeed. Those sorts of business connections are priceless.

Present Best Practices, Standardization, And Consistency.

Outsourcing content creation causes you to keep up a significant level of value all through long ventures and over a wide range of content. On the off chance, composting isn't your solid suit, staying up with the latest with best practices –

or in any event, recognizing what best practices are – can be intense.

At the point when you Outsourcing to a blog composing administration or other novel content makers, the authors taking a shot at your undertakings are for the most part experts who realize how to keep up the institutionalization that is urgent to marking, notoriety, and fruitful content showcasing.

A few quality checks, updates, proposals, and exacting adherence to your organization style manage to mean your Outsourcing content will be more than elegantly composed. It will be successful and superbly coordinated to your business.

In case you're as yet not persuaded about the advantages of Outsourcing, there are more motivations for outsourcing your blog and article advertising.

Do you utilize a blog composing administration to outsourcing a portion of your exceptional content needs? Why or why not?

The craft of incredible copywriting has changed. Quality content matters like never before. It makes a difference to shoppers who anticipate that organizations should deliver a normal stream of important content. It makes a difference to web crawlers that search for the privilege SEO sign to work out if the duplicate on the page answers search inquiries. Not constantly, asset or aptitudes to create this duplicate in-house. On the off chance, you are building your content methodology and pondering Outsourcing your copywriting.

Where To Find People To Outsource Tasks

As your business develops, so does your requirement for capable specialists. It very well may be a test to locate the ideal individuals to extend your group, also the financial backing to add them to your activities. Independent laborers offer your organization the chance to work with skilled people on the particular tasks you need them for. You can downplay your overhead while additionally accessing the ranges of abilities you requirement for the venture to turn out great.

Re-appropriating can be overpowering from the outset – every one of these destinations utilizes an alternate framework, have an alternate format and can take days to become acclimated to.

Choosing which site to utilize while finding some kind of harmony between aggressive rates and compelling outcomes can resemble strolling a virtual tightrope.

On the off chance, modest specialist locales are not feasible, where would you be able to discover great assistance to procure?

It is difficult, for the most part in light of the fact, the best consultants never at any point search for work — it comes to them.

In the event, conceivable, start by approaching companions and colleagues for referrals. That is the main way you'll arrive at the absolute best consultants.

Regardless of whether you're searching for the generously compensated, best independent occupations, or simply to get independent work as an afterthought that can help cushion your investment funds or cover the tabs, at that point you've gone to the ideal spot.

Regardless of if it's more bills than expected to wait to be addressed, your manager deteriorating, or in case you're simply tired of your full-time gig, I have your back with these best independent employments sites.

One of the most widely recognized holds back you'll hear is that it requires some investment to develop an outsourcing profession. You have to put resources into yourself, regardless of whether it be classes, programming, or marking. You have to make associations, you have to begin with lower-paying work to develop a portfolio and get your name out there.

Better believe it, the entirety of that is valid. Be that as it may, that doesn't mean you can't begin now. Like, RIGHT NOW.

Because it requires some investment to develop an independent business doesn't mean you can't get moving right now and make a plunge. So I incorporated this rundown of independent places of work that you can begin on immediately.

1. LinkedIn, AngelList

"There are numerous sites to discover skilled consultants. Customarily, we look to our very own systems, and to LinkedIn and Angel.co, to discover accessible and gifted specialists who can deal with a specific workstream or task. On these destinations, you can discover foundation data, tributes, and data about ranges of abilities." – Arry Yu, StormX

2. Upwork, Freelancer, Fiverr

Upwork is the aftereffect of a merger among Elance and oDesk, both viewed as pioneers in internet outsourcing before. Upwork markets itself as the world's biggest independent ability commercial center.

Consultants on Upwork make profiles sketching out their abilities and encounters, alongside their activity narratives and portfolios. Customers post-work postings specifying their tasks and what they're searching for in a consultant.

From that point, specialists submit recommendations for ventures they're keen on doing. Customers can audit consultants' recommendations, profiles, and portfolios, pick the one that best meets their requirements, and spot venture financing retained.

Specialists and customers at that point team up through an online work station, commonly with no off-platform correspondence.

All employments on Fiverr cost—you may figure this—$5, or in augmentations of $5. Fiverr is ideal for those simply beginning and hoping to construct a portfolio quickly.

In contrast to some different stages, customers and consultants can post postings—so a customer may have an occupation titled "Keep in touch with one 300-word article" while a specialist's adaptation would state "Will think of one 300-word article."

Fiverr spotlights on micro-jobs, such as composting or altering short articles or modifying bits of WordPress code.

Like Upwork, you can make a consultant profile and start offering on employments posted by customers.

Freelancer.com flaunts in excess of 29 million clients starting in 2019. Be that as it may, it tends to be hard to discover lucrative work there.

It's a decent decision for the individuals who want to work remotely and consider making the plunge in independent commercial centers.

3. Remote job boards

"Since we work for a completely remote organization, we like to post employments on remote-explicit destinations. A portion of our go-to locales has been RemoteWorkHub.com and FlexJobs.com. We've had great achievement discovering top ability whose No. 1 wanted advantage is having the option to work from anyplace." – Jared Atchison, WPForms

4. Craigslist

"It might appear to be old fashioned, however numerous individuals are astonished by how successful re-appropriating through Craigslist can be. It's one of my best three outsourcing destinations. I've utilized it to effectively Outsourcing composing, improvement, client service, and the sky is the limit from there. The key is to utilize early channels in your application procedure to eliminate commotion (like referencing a watchword in the subject of their application)." – Ruben Gamez, Docsketch

When utilizing Craigslist in your quest for new employment, try to altogether read the posts and adhere to the guidelines for applying. In the event, there are none, send an email with an introductory letter and resume to the email address alongside "Answer to this post" at the top.

5. Scripted

"It's a hit and miss when contracting content scholars, and the whole preparing period takes a couple of months. The entirety of this makes the content group quite costly to oversee. We enlist content scholars from Scripted, which opens up a huge amount of the board time, just as causes us to convey increasingly content without settling on quality." – Rahul Varshneya, Arkenea

6. Indeed

"Indeed gives access to some great specialists who will, in general, have more understanding. It's been an extremely effective asset regarding finding the correct blend of abilities for either remote or on location-independent staff." – Angela Ruth, Calendar

7. Industry-specific sites

"Since we work a lot of modules in the WordPress domain, I have discovered that locales identified with the WordPress people group have created a portion of my best contracts. A few destinations that we have utilized in our industry are WPHired.com and Jobs.WordPress.net. Investigate a portion of your industry-explicit destinations to discover higher-qualified competitors." – Syed Balkhi, WPBeginner

8. ProFinder by LinkedIn

"Did you realize that LinkedIn has a whole domain committed to independent work? It's called ProFinder, and it's isolated from the activity entryway. I've had the option to discover extraordinary specialists utilizing their administration since you're ready to see their whole resume, level of detachment and proposals." – Chris Christoff, MonsterInsights

9. Facebook and word of mouth

"While we have utilized numerous consultant sites throughout the years, from Elance to oDesk to Upwork to

Craigslist, my favored technique for re-appropriating ventures is informal. I like approaching individuals I know for proposals for consultants they have worked with firsthand on a comparative venture. In light of that, when I have a need, I bounce on Facebook and start making a few inquiries." – Adam Mendler, The Veloz Group

10. Toptal

"As I would see it, outsourcing ought to be insignificant in a startup or quickly developing the organization. There are some low-quality specialists locales, however just a couple with the greater part of them being skilled consultants. Toptal has the most excellent specialists. They highly esteem offering the best 3 percent of independent ability, and they are exceptionally prohibitive with the organizations and laborers that system in the stage." – Brian Condenanza, Alchemy Coin

Which site is ideal?

So, it relies upon the kind of work that you are doing.

For hourly work, Upwork is perhaps the best choice. For one-off task-based work, Guru and Freelancer.com are incredible choices as they have a procedure where you transfer assets into escrow (giving the supplier and consolation).

Arguments about finished work are typically taken care of quickly – in spite of the fact, it's imperative to have a reasonably expected set of responsibilities (see beneath – Tips for posting occupations). As far as we can tell Freelancer is best for getting venture based work finished.

Master is extraordinary on the off chance, you are searching for a US-based supplier. With Upwork the suppliers frequently need to pay to offer on ventures. This gives a bar that kills a portion of the lower quality suppliers. The outcome is that you are bound to pay somewhat more, however you are likewise bound to get a decent final product. Spots like Fiverr have laborers everywhere throughout the world, yet the costs are additionally more than reasonable.

On the off chance, you are searching for a particular kind of work, DesignHill and MTurk are increasingly engaged. These may be an extraordinary spot to begin in the event, you comprehend what you need, and need to just contract a planner, for instance.

It's difficult to state which site is the best since it relies upon your inclinations, your objectives, your spending limit, and how you like to work with telecommuters.

Each outsourcing site is unique, and you'll get various highlights, various advantages, various kinds of telecommuters, and diverse abilities. The best thought is to look at them all and see what works best for you separately.

Hourly versus Project:

By and large, you can contact either on a task premise, paying for a finished undertaking, or on an hourly premise.

Undertaking work is commonly more secure for you as there is a fixed sum you have to pay to get the errand complete.

At the point when you contract on an hourly rate, you don't have any consolation of the most extreme sum that you will spend.

An hourly rate is increasingly proper for longer-term work or where you have a wide range of errands for the individual.

Contracting:

On these destinations, there are commonly 2 sorts of laborers – people and groups.

The benefit of contracting an individual is that you know precisely who you are working with and you can get acquainted with the working style of that individual.

On the off chance, you are working long haul on an hourly rate, you can arrange lower rates on the off chance, you are working legitimately.

You will likewise have more control in the event, you are procuring an individual as opposed to you contracting an organization that has various workers. Then again an organization may bring all the more preparing, cooperative energy and a domain where individuals can request counsel and course.

As far as we can tell working with an individual is a superior move particularly in the event, you are cooperating in the long haul.

Tips for choosing the correct specialist

A typical battle with internet re-appropriating is winding up with individuals that can't take care of business or leave part of the way through a task.

One approach to conquer this issue is to employ individuals that have great criticism and appraisals. In the event, we are posting unpredictable employment, we never enlist anybody with under 30 finished occupations and they should have evaluations of higher than 90% (or 9 out of 10).

Another approach to analyzing your candidates is to maintain a strategic distance from any nonexclusive reactions. On the off chance, somebody hasn't tended to your criteria in a reasonable and basic manner, it's most likely not worth taking a gander at their work history.

You can even place a straightforward test part of your expected set of responsibilities like "notice the word elephant when you are answering with the goal that I realize you've readd our set of working responsibilities in full".

Posting Project Description:

1. Write your depiction as though you are disclosing them to a multi-year old youngster

2. Set clear achievements on the off chance, you need to use them for installments

3. Ask another person to read your undertaking portrayal before transferring it – in some cases, things that sound good to you will look bad to somebody who has no inclusion with your task or organization

4. Invite laborers who have coordinating experience. For example, in the event, you are searching for Joomla help, look for laborers with Joomla experience and great appraisals. Sort them by the last sign in date and afterward welcome them to your undertaking.

5. If you are stressed over ensuring your licensed innovation or thought, make an NDA and ensure you are trading it with a genuine element. Make your terms and conditions sensible (the majority of these locales have a standard NDA you can alter).

6. If you would prefer not to cause to notice what you are doing, keep your expected set of responsibilities dubious and examine subtleties just with parties you are keen on working with.

7. Post most of your expected set of responsibilities in a connection and leave a little "test" to ensure the individual has readd the depiction (for instance, referencing a specific word or requesting that they

address 2-3 key criteria).

8. Use assistance like gomockingbird.com to obviously lay out your thoughts in a visual medium

9. Make your task sound energizing and incorporate that it will glance great in any portfolio

10. Post your business to explicit geographic locales relying on the kind of laborer you are searching for.

Instruments TO HELP YOU MANAGE FREELANCERS EFFECTIVELY

There's an incredible article additionally on this site with a total rundown of the best instruments to oversee consultants.

I'm not going to go over that here, yet rather rapidly diagram the sorts of devices you ought to think about utilizing:

- A specialized instrument: guarantee you and whoever you contract can rapidly speak with one another as essential. Email is alright, however, Skype or Slack can accelerate reactions on each side.

- A venture arranging instrument: Trello or Google Docs can enable you to spread out your undertaking unmistakably, and let your specialist keep you refreshed of issues or progress.

- A screen recording apparatus: this isn't fundamental in the event, you enlisted a legitimate specialist. In any case, on the off chance, you went for a modest alternative, a screen recording instrument will ensure there are no disasters with timesheets.

Remote work is becoming a practical, less expensive, and regularly better alternative with regards to building your group. Outsourcing can be astonishing or tragic relying upon how you go about it. On the off chance, you think about everything in this guide, you'll have a vastly improved possibility of discovering achievement.

Giving you outsourcing the correct work, clarify your necessities unmistakably, and guarantee that you convey, there's no motivation behind why you can't cut your outstanding task at hand without losing the things that make your business one of a kind.

How To Update The Blog On A Daily Basis

A great many posts are composed, seen by a couple of individuals and afterward disposed of into the blog entry burial ground.

This is an epic waste.

In case you're not directing people to your old blog entries, you are slicing your ROI drastically.

It doesn't bode well to spend loads of hours or several dollars making another blog entry and afterward allowing it to kick the bucket when it moves off your first page.

Your content advertising should, in any case, get indexed lists and site design improvement from more seasoned posts. Truth be told, a prepared blog entry can produce natural traffic.

The response to expanding your blog's traffic is most likely something straightforward that you as of now have: old blog entries. In the event, you've been blogging for a moment, you most likely have huge amounts of posts sitting in your documents that are simply hanging tight for some TLC to breathe life into them back. Envision if every one of your more seasoned posts got only 10 new guests for each day — that could signify equivalent significant development for your blog. In the present post, I'm discussing the tips and deceives I've as of late executed myself, which have been a huge assistance in getting TNC seen by more individuals.

Consider it along these lines: If another guest discovers your most recent blog entry and preferences, they haven't seen the other 99% of your blog entries. Do you imagine that they could profit from those posts?

Accepting that they're great posts, obviously, they might want them.

It does not just bode well to take advantage of your old content, yet it's best for your new readers also.

Which Posts Should You Update?

OK, so you've acknowledged that you should refresh a portion of your old posts. So which ones would it be a good idea for you to refresh?

The most evident content to refresh is your most noteworthy traffic posts. These posts are the no doubt ones your rivals will try to copy; the more extraordinary content you can add to them and the more modern you can keep them, the further you will be on top of things.

After your most elevated dealt posts, occasional posts can be a major success. A month or two early, update the post with new data and streamline it for the present year. It should then show up in the list items as of late refreshed.

Profoundly shared presents are great focuses on updates. These posts clearly performed well before; a bit of tweaking and refreshing might be everything necessary to dispatch the following influx of social offers (and traffic!). You can utilize an apparatus like Buzzsumo to find your most shared content from the previous year.

For what reason Should You Update Old Posts?

In the event, you've never contacted a post in the wake of hitting the Publish button, refreshing old posts likely appears to be odd to you. Will, anybody sees it? In what capacity will anybody realize you refreshed the post? What's the point?

It's working more astute instead of harder. Utilizing less vitality than it would take to create a totally new blog entry, you can refresh your old posts and help them gain considerably more traffic, online networking shares, and possibly more money.

This works, above all else, on the grounds that Google esteems freshness. The web search tool realizes that for certain inquiries, searchers truly need the most up to date data accessible.

Simply consider it. In case you're looking to see who won the Superbowl, you would prefer not to realize who won in 2012. On the off chance, you are inquiring about to purchase another advanced camera, you would prefer not to recognize what cameras were the best in 2008. You need to recognize what cameras are the best at this point. You as a searcher are bound to tap on results that vibe "later" − perhaps the ebb and flow year is a piece of the feature, or the outcome shows a date inside the most recent couple of months. Since you esteem that freshness does as well, Google; after some time, fresher outcomes are bound to sit higher in the outcomes.

Some of the time, it is easy to refresh a post since you can simply bring marginally outdated data state-of-the-art. On different occasions, the way to "freshness" isn't so clear. Here are a few different ways to refresh your old blog entries to make them crisp once more.

Stay up with the latest

The clearest approach to refresh an old post is, well, to refresh it. As much as we take a stab at evergreen content, that is, content that stays important after some time, there will undoubtedly be a couple of things that have gone stale.

116

Information, measurements, and studies are a genuine model. Without a doubt, that 2012 investigation was superbly fine to utilize when you composed this post in 2013, yet most likely in 2017, there is something more modern? Maybe a more current investigation has even arrived at an alternate resolution, making for a fascinating turn to add to your blog entry.

Screen captures are something else that can go stale rapidly. On the off chance, your post is an instructional exercise or some sort of how-to, odds are you've incorporated a couple of screen captures. Has the subject of the instructional exercise been refreshed with another interface? Consider supplanting the screen captures with more current ones, particularly if this is a profoundly dealt post, or it is defenseless against somebody tagging along and just making a more cutting-edge instructional exercise.

At long last, it tends to be sufficient just to attach a couple of additional passages handling ongoing advancements on a theme. For whatever length of time that the progressions to the post are significant, it ought to be sufficiently signed to Google that there is crisp data here to creep.

Adjust OLD TITLES TO BE MORE SEO-FRIENDLY

While they might be charming, titles like "Ongoing Musings" or "A Few Fun Tips for Your Friday" won't help your web index rankings. The title of your post is one of the most significant pieces of its SEO invitingness, so on the off chance, you need to rank higher in web crawlers, it's imperative to utilize titles that incorporate your catchphrases and sound fascinating enough to click. The most ideal approach to improve titles? Attempt to think about the precise expressions somebody would scan for so as to discover your post and remember them for your title.

Include More Information

Now and again the main update a post need is more. This is particularly valid for list posts. Possibly your rundown of 30 was the greatest, best rundown around three years prior when you composed it. Yet, in the event, the query items are covered with list posts with 50, 75, or even 100 things, it may be an ideal opportunity to draw out the serious weapons and compose a significant update. All things considered, looked with two rundown posts on a similar theme, OK click the one with 30 things, or 100?

Include Better Imagery

Do your more established posts get a ton of their traffic from Pinterest or Facebook? In the event, they do, refreshing the pictures to something significantly all the more engaging – or including symbolism, if there is none by any stretch of the imagination – can be an enormous success.

To give your post a lift on Pinterest, the least demanding activity includes a representation shape picture with an engaging photograph and the name of the post overlaid. This kind of symbolism does very well on Pinterest. What's more, there's no compelling reason to purchase stock photographs; in the event, you don't have your own photography for the post, there are a lot of free, excellent photographs accessible on the web. You can utilize a device like Canva to overlay the content. Remember to utilize Pinterest bunch sheets to develop your blog's audience.

To make your post additionally engaging on Facebook, you can add open chart meta labels to your post that consequently pull in a picture for sharing on the social stage. You need not do any coding. Probably the simplest approach to join a Facebook picture is utilizing the Yoast SEO module, which you may as of now have introduced.

Improve Your SEO.

While basic SEO changes individually may not be sufficient to trigger a "freshness" support from Google, on the off chance, you are refreshing the post in any case you should give your SEO a little TLC.

First stop: your essential watchword. This is the catchphrase you have connected to your SEO module, (for example, the Yoast SEO module just referenced). Do you have one? Does the watchword bode well? Have you utilized it in your title, meta portrayal, a header tag, and a couple of spots all through your content? (Don't watchword stuff – you simply need to utilize it a couple of times, normally.)

Next, check your pictures. Do they have an alt label set? Pinterest utilizes your alt tag as a depiction for your pin, of course, so you unquestionably need some important content there!

Pursue different proposals gave by your SEO module to customized direction on what different changes you could make to your post's site design improvement.

Incorporate Internal Links to Newer Content

This is another little however relentless change. Adding pertinent inward connects to your more established content can keep your guests moving around your site. The greater part of your site's interior connections presumably point back in time as opposed to advance, so this is an extremely significant advance and one that you should take each time you update old posts.

Edit for mistakes and dead links

On the off chance, you have to know one thing about SEO, it's this: web indexes are consistently on the chase for the BEST content out there. Consequently, if a post has spelling mistakes or connections that don't work, you'll lose some road cred in Google's look. Utilize a spell checker on old posts and read through them for evident blunders. Additionally, utilize a module like this one to locate any wrecked connections on your site. At that point, obviously, fix them!

Improve readability

In conclusion, plan to improve your site's comprehensibility. Online journals and sites do best if passages are separated into littler pieces of content. Attempt to keep each section to around 5-6 lines, instead of an enormous square of 15 sentences bunched together. At the point when readers navigate to read your old posts, you need to boost their perusing involvement to put it plainly, simple-to-understand sections.

Improve the post's meta depiction.

Survey the post's meta depiction. Is it still precise? Would you be able to refresh it to make it somewhat catchier? Keep in mind, meta portrayals don't influence the positioning of your content, yet they can affect its clickthrough rate from search. Ensure your meta portrayal is both a precise impression of what's inside the post and sufficiently tempting to get searchers to navigate to your content from indexed lists.

Republish it!

Yahoo! At this point, you ought to have a marvelously refreshed bit of content that is prepared for distributing. While the procedure of really distributing your content will shift contingent upon the blogging programming you use, I'm going to share a few hints for doing it utilizing HubSpot's Blogging apparatus.

- Replace the old content with new content. This will likely be the equivalent regardless of what programming you use. Like I referenced, I typically duplicate/glue the HTML from my new draft to supplant the duplicate in my unique article.

- Wait until you need to distribute the "new" post to refresh its date/time. In case you're utilizing HubSpot's new Blog COS, you'll need to hold up until the particular date/time you need the post to show up on your blog landing page to click "update." Changing it to a date/time, later on, will bring about a 404 blunder for the individuals who discover the article in search before the recently assigned distribute date/time (not something to be thankful for if your article as of now positions well in indexed lists).

- Send a manual email to moment supporters. On the off chance, your blogging programming is (or resembles) HubSpot, it will just trigger the programmed email warning to supporters for a post once. This implies in case you're simply changing the distribute date/time on an effectively live article, the email won't get activated once more. In any case, in case you're utilizing HubSpot's new Blog COS, there's no preventing you from making a manual notice email in HubSpot's Email device and sending it to your moment endorser list. In the event, you utilize a similar layout you use for your programmed messages, your supporters won't have the option to differentiate. Additionally, you can utilize the chance to run an A/B test!

Track the previously/after execution.

Alright - possibly I lost track of what's most important. Before you distribute your new post, it's a smart thought to make a record of the post's "previously" details. That way, you can contrast it with the post's exhibition after you've republished it to see how your update influenced its general execution. After some time, this may likewise give you a superior thought regarding which posts merit focusing for refreshes. Coming up next are the information and details I monitor when I republish:

- Post's Title (on the off chance, I change it for the republished adaptation)

- Post's URL (to make sure I have the data in a single spot)

- Before/After Publish Dates

- Before/After Number of Comments

- Before/After Number of Inbound Links

- Before/After Number of Social Shares (for example Facebook, LinkedIn, Twitter, Google+, and so forth.)

- Before/After Post Views (utilize the prior month and the month after as an intermediary)

- Before/After New Contacts/Leads Generated (utilize the prior month and the month after as an intermediary)

- Before/After Keyword Rankings

Ideally, since you've readd this post, you have a couple of blog entries of your own as a main priority to refresh. Refreshing old blog entries is an extraordinary chance to work more intelligent as opposed to harder, so make certain to make a move.

Tips:

Here are the tips, condensed:

- Why would it be advisable for you to refresh old posts? Since freshness is an important characteristic, one that Google will organize in indexed lists.

- How do you pick which presents on update first? Organize posts that get a great deal of traffic, are occasionally applicable, or that have gotten a ton of offers previously. Next, center around your "speedy successes," those pages that are positioning lower than the best scarcely any list items for aggressive terms.

- How would it be a good idea for you to refresh your posts? Bring the data modern, include increasingly content, include more pleasant pictures, improve your SEO, and incorporate inside connections to more current content.

A large portion of these tips are intended to build blog traffic by streamlining your Pinterest and SEO control, however, once you improve your more seasoned content, there's such a significant number of different ways you can use it! You could share those spruced up posts in bulletins, add them to a "mainstream posts" segment on your sidebar, utilize a re-worked form as a visitor post, transform them into a free digital book for supporters, and the sky is the limit from there. Be inventive!

Conclusion:

Whether you are a beginner blogger or a professional one. You might have some questions to get the answers in order to improve your blogging skills or to start from the beginning with a complete guideline. Therefore, this guide was primarily designed to provide you with great assistance to learn and make you aware of the key factors that are required to be considered in every aspect of blogging. Regardless of an individual's personal concern. This guide has significantly aimed to help you with every aspect which ranges from selecting a topic to registering your own domain.

An ever-increasing number of organizations are getting into the content game. This has made a business opportunity for keen authors who can compose for a particular audience. Some have a reasonable methodology, while others are simply getting on board with the fleeting trend and trusting it pays off down the line.

You need to consider while you start writing your blog, but here, in this guide, these factors will be discussed in detail. You can make it as beneficial as you need it to be. You will need to have a platform that is anything but difficult to utilize and gives you the customization devices you are searching for to give your group of spectators all that they have to read and cooperate with your blog.

Search engine optimization necessities continue changing, and it tends to be difficult to stay aware of the most recent advancements. Be that as it may, on the off chance, you need your site to get traffic, you must be up to date. As far as I can tell, a couple of little changes can greatly affect rankings, particularly if the page wasn't all-around upgraded in the first place.

The main specialties you ought to consider on the off chance, you truly need to bring home the bacon with your blog. You must remember, your readers aren't destined to be keen on every one of the themes you actually love.

You need solid and qualified inquiry traffic however don't have a clue where to start, this post will be your best asset. Read it strictly and follow up on the pearls that you find.

Weblogs are likely the nearest advanced comparable to customary diaries on the Internet. A weblog can be comprehended as an innovative instrument just as a type of individual and social practice. As a mechanical device, it is a moderately simple to-utilize web-content administration framework that encourages the advancement and upkeep of a sequentially organized site that requires visit refreshing.

"Bloggers are headed to report their lives, express profoundly felt feelings, articulate thoughts through composition, and shape and keep up network forums". Blogs can be composed of various audiences and with various permeability alternatives. Passages can be either private or secret phrase ensured for a particular audience or totally open to the web. They can be composed exclusively or cooperatively. At the point when open, websites furnish bloggers with a feeling of composing for an audience of people and allowing readers the chance to add critiques beside the first posting or responding inside their own weblog by including a trackback connect.

In the course of the most recent decade, blogging has advanced from having increasingly close to home to progressively proficient objectives. Rather than people exclusively blogging for their loved ones, blogging started to envelop experts blogging for the general population to advance their own image and their business.

Web-based life audiences are more open to blog entries than they are advertisements or deals pages, and similarly, are bound to share blog entries with their associations than promotions or deals pages. By making blog content, you give yourself more to share on your online networking profiles, and you give your guests something to share when they visit your site. Social sharing of your content will expand the introduction to your intended interest groups and lead to progressively approaching traffic.

As you may definitely know, blogging has been helping numerous individuals and organizations in the course of the last 10-15 years. The facts confirm that more than two decades back, blogging barely existed. Today, there are a huge number of web journals online everywhere throughout the world!

Yet, despite everything we get fomented attempting to persuade individuals about the advantages of blogging. Regardless of whether profiting on the web is anything but an essential objective, the blog could help from various perspectives. We should take a gander at all the rewards bloggers get.

The two individuals and organizations have their data posted on the web. What happens then when somebody looks through your name? One of the benefits of websites is that it enables you to assemble and to control your online personality.

Besides interpersonal organization profiles, individuals who are looking for your name can discover your blog or your creator page on different websites. That data will help individuals to become acquainted with you better by perusing your work.

You did not just train others when you blog. You learn too. From the start, you will become familiar with your specialty since you have to instruct yourself to educate others. You will likewise gain proficiency with a ton about different fields, for example, web-based promoting, regardless of what you compose.

In any case, there's a sure measure of promoting information you should build the traffic to your blog. Your insight into email showcasing, internet searcher advertising, and online networking promoting will keep on developing.

Probably the best advantage of blogging is interfacing with others. You don't simply develop a few adherents on informal communities or email records. You assemble real connections. You befriend individuals you wouldn't have met something else.

On the off chance, you love voyaging, blogging likewise encourages you to take a brief trip and see the magnificence of the world. You can do all these while as yet getting a charge out of an unassuming living from blogging!

Everything entrepreneurs ought to be done intentionally. Don't simply write to compose. Consider who your clients are and what they need. Consider the reasons why a blog could support your business. Find what your clients are looking for and afterward convey.

Finding an extraordinary voice in your blog falls under marking techniques for your business. There are a million different ways to state something, attempt to discover a voice that resounds with your objective clients.

Blogging manufactures trust. Alongside internet based life, your blog is the human point of your business. Blogging constructs trust by additionally displaying your business' information.

In spite of the fact, the general public around the blogosphere is disappearing and blogging rehearses are getting progressively differing with the pervasiveness of interpersonal organizations, questions in regards to explicit uses for specific purposes.

As the web and innovation become progressively imbued in our everyday lives, the advantages of blogging or building a site become difficult to overlook. Be that as it may, not at all like in the good 'old days, bloggers don't have to have software engineering degrees or HTML information. Programming, for example, WordPress.org and "how to begin a blog" guides have made it basic and simple to set up a blog shortly. In case you're uncertain of in the case of blogging is directly for you, utilize a free blogging platform for a couple of months before changing to a self-facilitated arrangement.

Without wasting a single minute, start your blog today to start earning!

www.ingramcontent.com/pod-product-compliance
Lightning Source LLC
LaVergne TN
LVHW052302060326
832902LV00021B/3666